Using Statistics in Science Projects, Internet Enhanced

Melanie Jacobs Krieger

Enslow Publishers, Inc.

40 Industrial Road   PO Box 38
Box 398   Aldershot
Berkeley Heights, NJ 07922   Hants GU12 6BP
USA   UK

http://www.enslow.com

To my husband, Allen,
and my children, Tara and Stevn:
the best statistics in the world!

Library of Congress Cataloging-in Publication Data

Krieger, Melanie Jacobs, 1944–
    Using statistics in science projects, Internet enhanced / Melanie Jacobs Krieger.
      p. cm. — (Science Fair Success)
    Rev. ed. of: Means and Probabilities. c1996.
    Includes bibliographical references and index.
    Summary: Explains how to use statistics to interpret the data compiled
in a science project and suggests where to find additional information
on the Internet.
    ISBN 0-7660-1629-3
    1. Statistics—Juvenile literature. 2. Science—Experiments—Statistical methods—
Juvenile literature. [1. Statistics. 2. Science Projects.] I. Krieger, Melanie Jacobs, 1944–
Means and Probabilities. II. Title. III. Series.
QA276.13 .K75   2002
507'.8—dc21

                                    2001003424

Printed in the United States of America

10 9 8 7 6 5 4 3 2 1

To Our Readers:
We have done our best to make sure all Internet Addresses in this book were active and
appropriate when we went to press. However, the author and the publisher have no control over
and assume no liability for the material available on those Internet sites or on other Web sites they
may link to. Any comments or suggestions can be sent by e-mail to comments@enslow.com or to
the address on the back cover.

This book was originally published in 1996 by Franklin Watts as *Means and Probabilities: Using
Statistics in Science Projects.*

Photo Credits: Corel Corporation, p. 16; Enslow Publishers, Inc., pp. 18, 24, 48, 104,
112; Library of Congress, p. 31; Melanie Jacobs Krieger, pp. 7, 11, 44, 52, 66, 102, 118.

Cover Photo: Corbis Stock Market

Contents

Introduction

People usually think of numbers and mathematics as a very exact science. For instance, you can be quite sure that 2 + 2 = 4. You know that if you had 2 dollars and a friend gave you another 2 dollars, you would have 4 dollars. The solution to this problem is precise and easily understood. No interpretation is necessary. The basic methods that you learn in your math classes are problem-solving techniques that enable you to add dollars, inches, miles, and so on to obtain exact values as answers.

However, not everything in life is this simple. Many mathematical problems do not ask you to just add or subtract numbers, but rather ask you to collect, organize, analyze, and interpret numbers. This is when mathematicians turn to statistics for help.

For example, suppose you wanted to know whether the girls in the ninth grade of your school are better spellers than the boys, or vice versa. To find out, you would first give them a spelling test. You would then find the average score for each gender. Then you could compare the girls' average score to the boys' average score. But this is not always so easy. What if your results are as shown in Table 1?

Table 1. Spelling Scores for Ninth-Grade Students

	Average Score
Girls	87
Boys	85

At first glance, you might say that the girls are better spellers than the boys. But if you think about it, you might realize that the scores are really not that different. You might begin to wonder whether you could say with certainty that the girls are better spellers than the boys. After all, you would be able to argue that both scores would receive a B+ on a report card. Now you have a dilemma. You have two numbers that are definitely not the same yet are very close in value. Can you say this two-point difference is meaningful?

This is where statistical methods can help. *Statistics* can be used to determine whether the difference is meaningful, or significant. Once you learn statistical techniques, you will find that they are easy to use, and can help immensely in finding answers to important problems.

This is a practical, how-to book. It will show you how to use statistics to interpret the data you compile in a science project. You will find that using statistics adds greatly to the conclusions you can draw and the impression your project makes on the judges in science competitions.

The Scientific Method

Science research experiments can be very exciting projects. Each undertaking is a unique experience with the possibility of discovering something new and exciting. It may be new not only to you, but also to the science world!

If you have never done a science project, you will find that it is very different from a classroom lab project. In the lab, the teacher typically assigns a task or a project that lasts about thirty minutes. The teacher already knows the correct results of the task, and if your results are different from the expected ones, your experiment is usually considered a failure.

However, real science does not proceed this way. Scientists in the research laboratory do not know what their results will be. They work with hypotheses and unknowns. They seek the unexpected and the new. Quite often their experiments meet with failure, rather than success. But this is how science proceeds. Knowing what does not work leads scientists to try new things.

Scientists conduct projects that take as long as necessary—minutes, hours, days, and even years. As their experiments progress, scientists may revise their hypotheses in response to new information. There is no cookbook recipe as there is in a school laboratory. A scientist encounters many setbacks along with success.

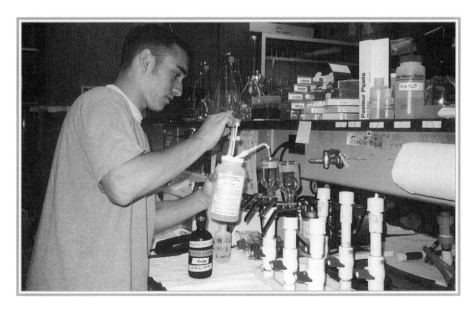

This student will use the scientific method while conducting a science project.

A science project should always follow the scientific method. The scientific method is a set of steps all scientists follow when conducting research experiments. If you follow these steps, you can create a project that would qualify for any of the prestigious science research competitions, such as the Intel Science Talent Search Competition. It might even be worthy of being published in a scientific journal.

The scientific method involves the following six steps:

1. **State a hypothesis.**

   A hypothesis is a statement asserting the problem you will be investigating in your experiment. As you work on your project, you hope to prove or disprove the statement. For example, a person conducting the spelling investigation discussed earlier might have a hypothesis that girls are better spellers than boys.

   Before you come up with a hypothesis, it is a good idea to read all the background information you can about your research topic. Remember to consult current periodicals, journals, and computer databases, as well as books. Try to discover whether other people have tried an experiment similar to the one you want to do. If so, look into the results they obtained.

   Now you are ready to formulate your own hypothesis, which is basically an educated guess about what your experiment will show. State the problem you will be investigating in your experiment.

2. **Design an experiment that will allow you to accept or reject the hypothesis.**

   Now that you have stated the problem, decide on the type of data you will need to collect and how you will gather it. Start by writing an outline of the procedures you plan to use. Write up a tentative schedule. Determine whether you must buy or borrow equipment and whether you will have to construct a special lab setup. If you will be working with live specimens, such as plants, figure out where you will store them and how you will care for them.

If your research involves vertebrate animals, human subjects, recombinant DNA, or animal tissue, learn the rules and fill out the appropriate forms. Discover the safety measures that you must take with your experiment. For projects involving human subjects, find out if you will need consent forms. For projects in the social science area, develop your questionnaire and define the subject pool you wish to test.

It is best to design your experiment so that only one variable at a time is being changed or tested. In this way, you can be more certain that any change in outcome is caused by the tested variable and nothing else. If too many things are changing at the same time, it may be difficult to understand how your variable affects the end result.

3. **Assemble the experimental set-up.**

   Assemble the equipment for your experiment. Test your equipment to make sure you can conduct your experiment without frequent breakdowns. If you are doing a project in the social sciences, create a survey form that you can use to question participants.

4. **Conduct your experiment and collect the data.**

   The *data* are the numbers you collect during your project. For instance, it may be the number of french fries in a fast-food serving, or the number of inches of rainfall per day. If your project involves a questionnaire, this is the time to give out the questionnaire and then collect the responses. The responses will be your data.

In carrying out your experiment, carefully follow the procedures you have planned. Do not be alarmed if you run into a number of problems with the equipment or lab setup. When that happens, simply modify your original plan. Your perseverance and ingenuity in solving these problems will demonstrate your talent as a scientist.

5. **Analyze the data, using statistical methods.**

   Analyze and interpret the data you have collected from your experiment. First, organize your data, using tables, charts, and graphs. Then, using the statistical methods explained in this book, interpret the data. Your analysis will enable you to make a scientific judgment as to whether you have proved or disproved your original hypothesis.

   You can carry out your statistical analysis with a calculator or one of the commercial statistical computer packages.

6. **Write and publish the paper.**

   Your work is not complete until you write up your results and share them with other scientists and researchers.

   The advantage of the scientific method is that it allows you to develop a hypothesis and then prove it or disprove it in a logical and straightforward manner. Statistics is an essential part of this process. It allows you to analyze and interpret the data that you collect during the course of your experiment.

Understanding Statistics

This book will start by showing you how to arrange data in graphs and charts. You will then learn to calculate averages and other *descriptive statistics*. Descriptive statistics are values that describe some aspect of the data. Later, you will learn about statistics that help interpret data. They are called *inferential statistics* because they allow you to make inferences about a group of objects or people from the investigation of only a small sample of the group.

In most cases, it is impossible to study the entire group, or *population*, in an experiment. If you were studying oak trees, for example, you would not be able to study every oak tree in the world. If you attend a very large school, it might be difficult to test the spelling ability of all the ninth graders there. But you could choose a *sample* of students to

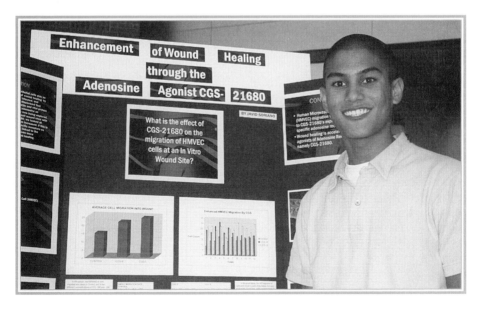

This student presents an award-winning science project, in which statistics were used to analyze the experimental data.

test that represents the entire population of ninth graders. You would make sure your sample included students from both honors and nonhonors classes to ensure that all levels of ability were represented.

If the sample is to accurately represent the entire population, it is very important that the items or individuals in the sample be chosen randomly. The easiest way to get a *random sample* for the spelling investigation would be to assign a number to every ninth grader. Then you would put all the numbers in a container, shake it up, and pull out numbers at random. A computer can also help you select random numbers.

The best way to learn statistical methods is to actually apply them to different problems. For that reason, there are many examples throughout the book. As you go through the examples, think about how the same techniques might be applied to your own projects.

Chapter 1

Organizing Data

Collecting data is an important aspect of every science project. It may sound like a simple thing to do, but if this is not done in a neat and organized manner, you may find it frustrating, if not impossible, to analyze and interpret your data. The best way to organize your data is to put it in a table.

Suppose you are measuring the acidity of the rainfall in your town from day to day. Your data table might look like Table 2.

Table 2. Data for Rainfall Experiment

	Rainfall	pH
Day 1	0.11	5.5
Day 2	0.34	4.5

A properly constructed table clearly summarizes a set of data. It presents information far more effectively than a sentence full of numbers. For instance, what if you wanted to list the five tallest mountains, with their heights and locations? If you wrote all this information in a sentence, you might have something like this:

The five tallest mountains in the world are: Mount Everest at 29,108 feet in the Himalayan Mountain Range in Nepal and Tibet; Mount Godwin Austin at 29,064 feet in the Karakoram Mountain Range in Kashmir; Mount Kanchenjunga at 28,208 feet in the Himalayan Mountain Range in Nepal and Sikkim; Mount Lhotse at 27,890 feet in the Himalayan Mountain Range in Nepal and Tibet; and Mount Makalu at 27,790 feet in the Himalayan Mountain Range in Tibet and Nepal.

This sentence contains a lot of information about the five tallest mountains in the world, but it is difficult to grasp quickly. You cannot easily see the relationship among the pieces of information. For instance, the following is not immediately obvious:

- The name of the tallest mountain in the world
- The location of the second tallest mountain
- The name of the mountain(s) found in Sikkim

Table 3 organizes all the information found in the sentence.

Table 3. The Five Tallest Mountains in the World

Mountain	Elevation (feet)	Location
Mount Everest	29,108	Himalayas in Nepal and Tibet
Mount Godwin Austin	29,064	Karakoram Range in Kashmir
Mount Kanchenjunga	28,208	Himalayas in Nepal and Sikkim
Mount Lhotse	27,890	Himalayas in Nepal and Tibet
Mount Makalu	27,790	Himalayas in Nepal and Tibet

The table was easier to create than the long clumsy sentence, and it is much easier to understand. You can immediately see that:

- The tallest mountain is Mount Everest, with an elevation of 29,108 feet.

- The second tallest mountain, Mount Godwin Austin, is found in the Karakoram Range in Kashmir.

- Part of Mount Kanchenjunga is in Sikkim.

You can also quickly see that four of the tallest mountains in the world are in the Himalayas. And with a quick calculation you can determine that the difference between the world's tallest mountain and the fifth tallest mountain is only 1,318 feet.

By the time you finish your science project, you will have collected a large amount of data. At first glance, your data values may appear random and spread out. Most likely, you will not have an instant picture of your experimental results. But if you arrange these numbers into a table or chart, you will have a format that is simple and easy to read.

A table will summarize the data and show you its *distribution*, or how your data is spread out over a range of values. Thus, you will be able to see clusterings and trends in the data. At a glance, you will be able to see the scores at the extremes and in the center of your distribution.

A table should be a self-contained body of information. All the columns must be clearly labeled and the title should be self-explanatory. This makes it possible to understand the results of the experiment just by reading the table title and then studying the table.

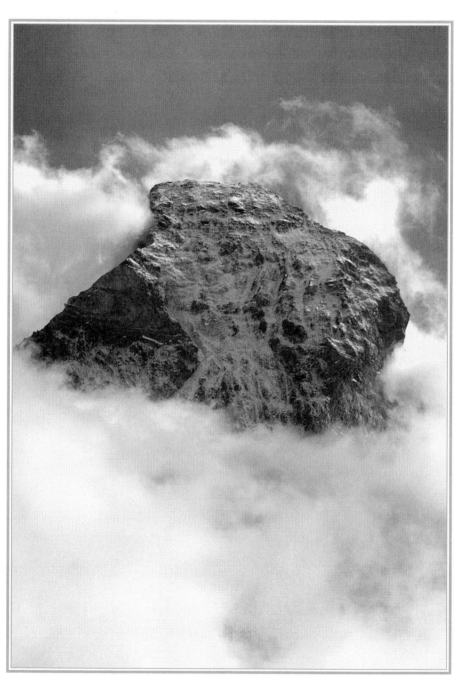

Mount Everest in the Himalayan Mountain Range is one of the five tallest mountains in the world.

Each table you create will be different depending on the type and the amount of data you have collected. Suppose you had surveyed 15 customers chosen randomly at Dave's Music Discs to find out how many compact discs they were buying. You might end up with the following 15 pieces of data:

$$1, 4, 5, 3, 2, 1, 4, 3, 2, 2, 1, 1, 2, 1, 3$$

This string of numbers is rather meaningless until you organize it in a table. Table 4 summarizes the data. If you examine the table briefly, it is fairly obvious that most customers bought either 1 or 2 CDs.

Table 4. Number of CDs Bought by Customers

Number of CDs purchased	1	2	3	4	5
Number of customers	5	4	3	2	1

Grouping Data

In many experiments, you may collect hundreds of pieces of data. A large number of values widely spread out can be unwieldy to work with. In such situations, it is often helpful to arrange the data in groups.

To demonstrate the advantage of this approach, let's take an example with 40 pieces of data. Suppose you wish to assess the mathematics abilities of the students in your high school by using scores on the math portion of the Scholastic Aptitude Test (SAT I).

You might go to the high school guidance office and randomly select 40 student files. The high school should withhold the identities of the students. It is best not to have this information so that you can remain objective. You record the 40 math SAT I scores as shown in Table 5.

Table 5. SAT I Scores from 40 Randomly Selected High School Students

770	670	580	720	680	500	520	610	500	490
600	560	600	570	610	630	700	500	540	640
560	550	650	670	640	530	520	580	610	600
470	650	570	600	550	660	640	510	520	500

(Note that the lowest possible Math SAT I score is 200 and the highest possible score is 800.)

As you look at these numbers, you will likely find that you are unable to determine anything about the math abilities of the students in your high school. Table 5 gives no indication as to the average score. But if you organize the scores in some logical way, they will have more meaning.

How many CDs do most customers buy?

Frequency Distribution

One approach is to list all possible scores, beginning with the highest and ending with the lowest of the 40 scores. Since SAT I scores are always multiples of 10, the list will include all multiples of 10 from 770 down to 470. If you place a slash mark next to each score every time it appears in Table 5, you will be able to see the distribution of scores. The number of slash marks represents the *frequency* of each score. See Table 6.

Table 6 is called an ungrouped frequency distribution of scores. Although you can now see that the data is spread widely among the scores in the table, the table still does not indicate the average score. Putting the scores into groups,

Table 6. Ungrouped Frequency Distribution of SAT I Scores of 40 High School Students

Scores					
770	/	660	/	550	//
760		650	//	540	/
750		640	///	530	/
740		630	/	520	///
730		620		510	/
720	/	610	///	500	////
710		600	////	490	/
700	/	590		480	
690		580	//	470	/
680	/	570	//		
670	//	560	//		

known as *class intervals*, will give you a better idea of where the average is and how the scores are distributed.

For this example, a good choice for the number of groups is 10. First, find the highest score in the list—770—and the lowest score in the list—470—and subtract the lowest from the highest:

$$770 - 470 = 300$$

There is a 300-point spread between the lowest and highest scores in this distribution. This spread is called the *range*.

Divide the range by 10, the number of groups, to find how many SAT I scores each group will cover:

$$300/10 = 30$$

Each group, or class interval, will cover 30 points. The first interval will range from a lower limit of 470 to an upper limit of 499. Notice that the difference between the upper and lower limit is only 29, but the number of points in the range is 30. If you have any doubt about this, count the points yourself. The next interval starts at 500 and ends at 529.

Find the remaining intervals by continuing this procedure of incrementing 1 for the lower limit and then adding 29 to get the upper limit. The last interval will have to contain 31 points to include 770. Now list the ten groups in decreasing order, as shown in Table 7.

Follow this general procedure whenever you are creating class intervals. It is always easier to start with the bottom interval and go up. Adding to a lower limit rather than subtracting from an upper limit will help you avoid careless mathematical errors.

To complete the grouped frequency distribution, mark the number of scores in each interval with slashes, as in Table 6.

Table 7. Class Intervals of SAT I Scores of 40 High School Students

Row Value	Lower Limit – Upper Limit
10	740 – 770
9	710 – 739
8	680 – 709
7	650 – 679
6	620 – 649
5	590 – 619
4	560 – 589
3	530 – 559
2	500 – 529
1	470 – 499

Write the total number of slashes in a new column, as shown in Table 8. This number is the frequency count in each interval. It is a good idea to check your work by adding up the frequency counts to make sure you have included all 40 data points.

The spread of the scores becomes much more obvious with this grouped *frequency distribution.* You can see that most of the scores are clustered in rows two to seven—the middle and lower end of the score range. But the first row and the last three rows, representing the lowest and highest scores, have only one or two scores apiece.

Thus, Table 8 displays the basic characteristics and trends of the SAT I score distribution, while also summarizing the data.

For any given situation, you must choose the number of classes based mainly on the amount of raw data you have. In

Table 8. Grouped Frequency Distribution of SAT I Scores

Row Value	Lower Limit – Upper Limit	Tally	Frequency (*f*)
10	740 – 770	/	1
9	710 – 739	/	1
8	680 – 709	//	2
7	650 – 679	/////	5
6	620 – 649	////	4
5	590 – 619	///////	7
4	560 – 589	000000	6
3	530 – 559	////	4
2	500 – 529	////////	8
1	470 – 499	//	2
			Total 40

most cases, it is best to put your data into 10 to 20 classes or groups. You want enough groups to show the spread of your data; if the intervals are too large, you risk losing too much information. Differences in the values of the original data are lost when the numbers are lumped together in just a few large groups.

But if there are too many groups with small intervals, the amount of information can be overwhelming. Too many groups defeat the purpose of grouping the data, which is to easily read, understand, and interpret it.

A More Precise Frequency Table

There are several other values that can help you define and interpret a frequency distribution. You can add this information to your frequency distribution by including several extra columns. The values in the columns will allow you to interpret your data in a more precise way, as well as to make accurate graphs of your data.

One helpful piece of information is called *true limits.* The true limits of a measured value are the lower and upper bounds of the measurement. If you weigh yourself on a scale, for instance, it may read 100 pounds, but do you really weigh exactly 100 pounds? Because of imperfections in the construction of the scale, you may weigh a bit more or a bit less than 100 pounds.

How much more or less? If the scale's display has increments of one pound, then you could weigh anywhere from 99.5 to 100.5 pounds and still have a reading of 100 pounds. These are the true limits of your weight measurements. Thus the true limits of a measurement can be obtained by taking half of the smallest increment on the scale display, and then both subtracting and adding that value to the measurement value. True limits are usually listed with class intervals, as shown in Table 9. The reason for defining true limit is so that every value will fall into only one class.

Another valuable statistic is the *midpoint* of the class. It is simply the center of the class interval, and can be calculated by adding the lower and upper class limits and dividing by 2.

Table 9. Examples of True Limits for Various Class Intervals

Class Intervals	True Limits
38–53	37.5–53.5
22.3–26.3	22.25–26.35

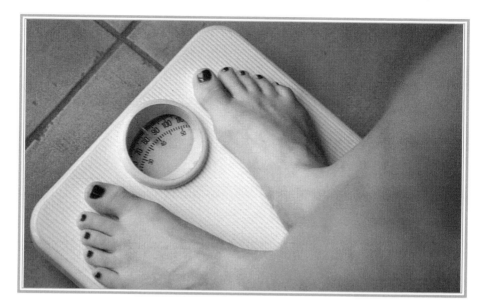

The reading you get on a weight scale may differ slightly from your actual weight depending on the true limits of the measurements.

Because the midpoint is often used to represent the entire class, it is sometimes called the *class mark*. The midpoints of some class intervals are given in Table 10.

In the example with the SAT I test scores, you figured the frequency of data values in each isolated class interval. Sometimes it is helpful to know how these frequencies accumulate as you progress from the lowest class to the highest. The statistic known as the *cumulative frequency*, or *cum f*, supplies this

Table 10. Examples of Midpoints for Various Class Intervals

Interval	Midpoint
4–6	5
85–91	88
123–130	126.5

Table 11. Cumulative Frequencies for a Set of Class Interval Scores (Note that *f* is an abbreviation for frequency and *cum f* an abbreviation for cumulative frequency.)

Class Interval	Midpoint	f	cum f
17–20	18.5	10	40
13–16	14.5	7	30
9–12	10.5	5	23
5–8	6.5	10	18
1–4	2.5	8	8

information. It is the sum of all the frequencies from the lowest class up to and including a given class. Table 11 shows the cumulative frequencies for a series of class intervals.

For the first class at the bottom of the table, the cumulative frequency is equal to the frequency, 8, because there are no lower classes. The cumulative frequency of the second class is 8 + 10 = 18. For the third class, *cum f* = 18 + 5 = 23, and so on. You will discover how useful the cumulative frequency can be in the section on percentiles.

The general procedure for organizing any set of data into a frequency distribution table with the columns of Table 11 is as follows:

1. Choose the number of class intervals.

2. Find a convenient class interval width.

3. Determine the lower and upper interval limits.

4. Determine the true limits for each interval.

5. Determine the midpoint of each interval.

6. Tally the data into the intervals.

7. Determine the frequency for each interval.

8. Put the data in a table and add a cumulative frequency column.

Now let's apply this procedure to a large set of data. Suppose you were interested in discovering how 100 randomly selected students performed on the last science test. The grades are shown in Table 12.

The first step is to divide the scores into 10 class intervals. Since the highest score is 99 and the lowest is 0, the spread of data is 99. If you divide 99 by 10 and round to the nearest whole number, you get a class width of 10.

Thus, the lower class limits will be: 0, 10, 20, . . . 90. And the upper class limits will be: 9, 19, 29, . . . 99.

Table 12. Science Test Scores for 100 Randomly Selected High School Students

12	98	54	76	94	33	76	56	76	87
34	21	58	78	93	56	93	78	87	50
56	53	97	98	99	78	98	93	82	39
78	73	32	87	56	93	83	93	81	93
90	82	47	84	86	84	89	97	99	84
11	43	21	83	82	87	82	89	95	78
0	91	38	48	82	85	72	88	96	40
65	95	12	79	91	82	28	77	68	73
75	63	97	94	73	98	59	70	39	79
87	99	32	84	59	54	27	68	60	94

To determine the true limits for these classes, you must know how the science teacher scored the tests. Let's assume that the teacher gave full-point credits for individual questions. The true limits would then be -0.5–9.5, 9.5–19.5, 19.5–29.5, and so on. Note that the upper class limit of the lowest class is equal to the lower class limit of the next class. This will become very important and useful in Chapter 2 when you graph your data.

To determine the midpoint of each class, subtract the lower class limit from the upper class limit and divide by 2: $(9 - 0)/2 = 4.5$. Therefore, 4.5 is the class mark or midpoint of the first interval. Note that even though 4.5 is the representative score for this interval, a score of 4.5 is not possible. Continue in the same way to find the midpoint of the other classes.

Tally the number of scores in each class and total them to obtain a frequency for each class interval. Then calculate the cumulative frequency for each class. You should now be able to organize your data as shown in Table 13.

If you study Table 13, you can see the entire distribution of scores. At a glance, you can tell the location of the extreme and central scores of your distribution. You can see that there are very few scores between 0 and 29 and many scores between 70 and 99. In fact, this distribution of scores is very lopsided. Most of the scores are clustered above 70 instead of in the middle of the distribution around the score of 50.

Thus, the frequency distribution table summarized the experimental results and displayed the basic characteristics and trends of the data. A teacher would find this information valuable because it could help pinpoint the best score to choose

Table 13. Complete Frequency Distribution for 100 Randomly Selected Science Scores (The frequency distribution includes class limits, true limits, midpoints, frequency, and cumulative frequency.)

Class	Class Limits	True Limits	Midpoint	f	Cum f
10	90–99	89.5–99.5	94.5	25	100
9	80–89	79.5–89.5	84.5	23	75
8	70–79	69.5–79.5	74.5	17	52
7	60–69	59.5–69.5	64.5	5	35
6	50–59	49.5–59.5	54.5	11	30
5	40–49	39.5–49.5	44.5	4	19
4	30–39	29.5–39.5	34.5	7	15
3	20–29	19.5–29.5	24.5	4	8
2	10–19	9.5–19.5	14.5	3	4
1	0–9	−0.5–9.5	4.5	1	1

as the passing grade. For instance, if 60 were the passing grade, 70 of the 100 students would pass the test. This could be determined by summing all the frequencies from class 7 and higher, since 60 is the lower limit of class 7. Adding all the frequencies in class 7 and up would give you 5 + 17 + 23 + 25 = 70. Or you could simply subtract the cumulative frequency for class 6 from 100. Can you see why this works?

Next, the frequency distribution will be used as the basis for constructing several types of graphs that will help you visually interpret your data.

Chapter 2

Graphing Data

In contrast to a table, a graph summarizes data from an experiment in a pictorial way. A pictorial presentation of data often exposes certain features that are not apparent in a frequency table. There are many types of graphs. Stem-and-leaf diagrams, pie charts, bar graphs, histograms, and frequency polygons are some of the more common. You must decide which one is best suited for your application.

As with tables, every graph needs a self-explanatory title, and the data must be clearly labeled.

Stem-and-Leaf Diagrams

Stem-and-leaf diagrams let you quickly see the shape or the spread of your data. Compared with other types of graphs, a unique feature of stem-and-leaf diagrams is that they include the actual numerical values of the collected data.

As an example, let's construct a stem-and-leaf diagram of the number of home runs Babe Ruth hit in each of his 15 years with the New York Yankees. Beginning with the year 1920 and ending with 1934, those values are:

54, 59, 35, 41, 46, 25, 47, 60, 54, 46, 49, 46, 41, 34, 22

To make a stem-and-leaf diagram, first arrange the data in increasing order. Then separate each piece of data into the 10s digit and the 1s digit. The 10s digits will form the stems of the diagram and the 1s digits will form the leaves.

List each stem value on one line, with the leaves to the right. For instance, a stem value of 2 would have two leaves to the right because there are two data values in the twenties: 22 and 25. So the leaves would be 2 and 5. It is best to arrange the leaves in increasing order, as shown in Table 14. Also, separate the stems and leaves with a vertical line.

From the stem-and-leaf diagram, you can immediately see that the range of home runs is 22 to 60. The smallest number of runs is 22, and the largest is 60. You can also see that stem 6 contains the fewest number of leaves. It has just one leaf. That tells you that Babe Ruth had only one season in which he hit 60 or more home runs.

Table 14. Stem-and-Leaf Diagram Showing the Yearly Number of Home Runs Babe Ruth Hit from 1920 To 1934

10s digit	1s digit
2	2 5
3	4 5
4	1 1 6 6 6 7 9
5	4 4 9
6	0

What information can a stem-and-leaf diagram tell you about Babe Ruth's home run record?

Stem 4, with 7 leaves, contains the most leaves. This means that most of the data is concentrated in the 40s. Babe Ruth hit between 40 and 50 home runs during seven seasons of play. The middle of the distribution, 46, is located on stem 4. It is the point at which there are an equal number of data points above and below it. Babe Ruth hit less than 46 home runs six of the years, more than 46 six of the years, and exactly 46 three of the years. So it is readily apparent that this group of data is centered at 46.

You can easily see the overall shape of the distribution, which is determined by how far the leaves extend to the right. The shape for this set of data is relatively *symmetric*. A distribution is symmetric if the portions above and below its middle are mirror images of each other. In this case, the distribution is not perfectly symmetric because the two upper stems have 2 leaves apiece, whereas the two lower stems have 3 and 1. If a distribution is far from being symmetric, it is *skewed*.

The diagram also shows that there are no gaps in the distribution, nor are there any *outliers*. An outlier is an extreme score that falls far outside the overall pattern of the data. An outlier could indicate an error—in recording the data, for instance—or it may simply represent a very unusual occurrence.

A stem-and-leaf diagram with an outlier is shown in Table 15. It displays the number of home runs Roger Maris hit during his ten years in the American League. The outlier is the 61 home runs he hit in 1961. This was an extraordinary year for him, since in most years he hit less than half that many. So Maris's record year is an outlier, an individual value that stands apart from his usual pattern.

Table 15. A Stem-and-Leaf Diagram of Roger Maris's Yearly Home Runs During Ten Years in the American League

10s digit	1s digit
0	8
1	3 4 6
2	3 6 8
3	3 9
4	
5	
6	1

Bar Graphs

Bar graphs consist of vertical or horizontal bars. The length of each bar represents the number of items in a category. Thus, the graph allows you to visually compare the quantities of categories. Suppose you want to display the voting pattern of a random sample of 100 voters taken during the election for mayor of Florida City. The results of the sample are shown in Table 16.

Table 16. Votes of 100 Randomly Selected Voters in the Florida City Mayoral Election

Candidates	Votes
Brown	25
Cho	41
Rivera	34

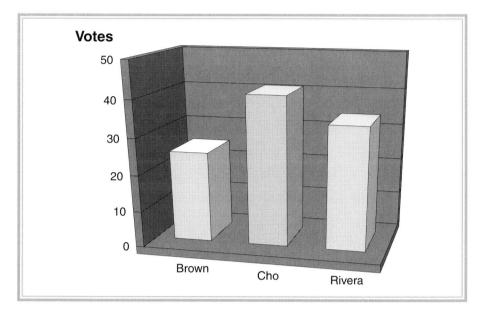

Figure 1: Bar graph showing the votes of 100 randomly selected voters in the Florida City mayoral election.

A bar graph of these results would look like Figure 1. This presentation allows you to see clearly and immediately the differences in the number of votes for each candidate. Note that the length of the bar represents the quantity that you wish to compare. The bars must be of uniform width and equally spaced. Note also that the bars are separated rather than touching. Bar graphs are suitable for situations in which the data "values" are not of a continuous numerical nature, but are completely separate items, such as the names of candidates in an election.

Histograms

A *histogram* is similar to a bar graph, but it is designed for data that covers a continuous range of numerical values. As a result, a histogram differs from a bar graph in two important ways. In a histogram, the bars always touch, whereas in a bar graph, they are separated. Secondly, you can make the bars in a bar graph as wide as you wish, to make the visual impression you want to convey. But in a histogram, the width of a bar represents a numerical value.

A histogram of the number of home runs that Babe Ruth hit in each of his 15 years with the New York Yankees is shown in Figure 2.

Notice that the histogram shows the shape of the distribution in the same way the stem-and-leaf diagram did. The stem-and-leaf diagram is somewhat like a histogram turned on its side.

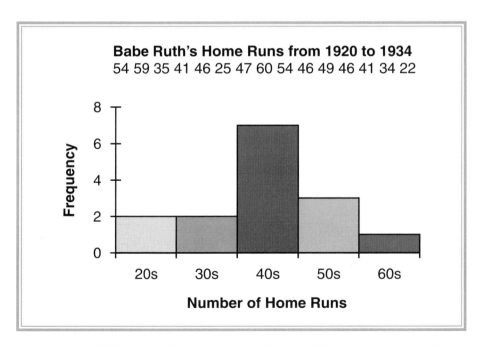

Figure 2: A histogram depicting the distribution of home runs Babe Ruth hit during his 15 years with the Yankees

To create a histogram:

1. Organize the data into a frequency distribution table as stated previously.

2. Draw the histogram using lower and upper true limits as the boundaries for each class on the horizontal axis and the frequency for each class on the vertical axis.

The histogram gives the impression that frequencies seem to jump suddenly from one class to the next. If you want to emphasize the continuous rise or fall of the frequencies, you can easily convert the histogram into a *frequency polygon.*

Frequency Polygons

A frequency polygon might be thought of as a histogram that has been turned into a line graph. It is made by connecting

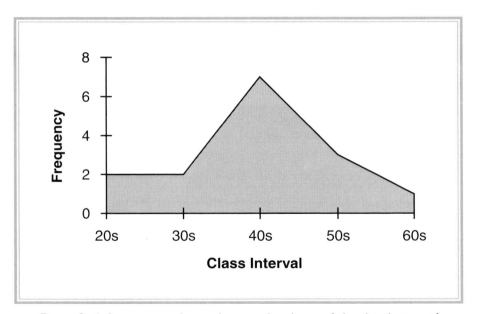

Figure 3: A frequency polygon showing the shape of the distribution of Babe Ruth's yearly home runs during his 15 years with the Yankees

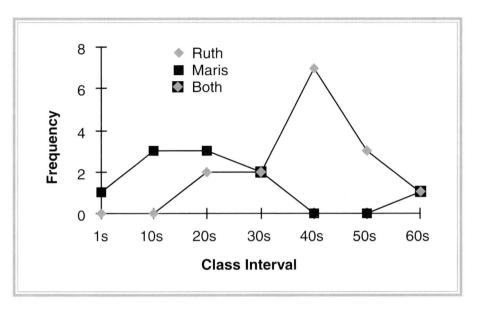

Figure 4: This frequency polygon compares the distributions of Babe Ruth's home run record from 1920 to 1934 (diamonds) to the distribution of Roger Maris's home run record during his ten years in the American League (squares). This graph enables you to see that Babe Ruth consistently hit 30, 40 and 50 home runs many times, while Roger Maris consistently hit 10, 20 and 30 home runs. This makes Babe Ruth's 60 home runs look like part of a very strong pattern, while Roger Maris's 61 home runs look more like an outlier.

the midpoints of the tops of the bars of the histogram. But a frequency polygon can be constructed without first drawing a histogram. Just plot the frequency of each class at the midpoint of the interval and connect the points.

A frequency polygon of Babe Ruth's home runs is shown in Figure 3.

Frequency polygons are especially useful for comparing two different distributions. The frequency polygon in Figure 4, for example, compares the distribution of home runs hit by Babe Ruth and Roger Maris.

Pie Chart

A graph drawn in the shape of a circle is known as a pie chart. Pie charts can be grasped quickly, and they can give a good overview of your collected data. They are especially useful for showing the component parts of a quantity.

The entire circle represents the total quantity—100 percent. Each wedge or pie slice of the circle represents some percentage of the total. A pie chart of Babe Ruth's home run record is shown in Figure 5. It was created by first converting the frequency counts to percentages of the total number of years, as shown in Table 17. Multiplying these percentages by 360 degrees then gives the size of the pie slice in degrees.

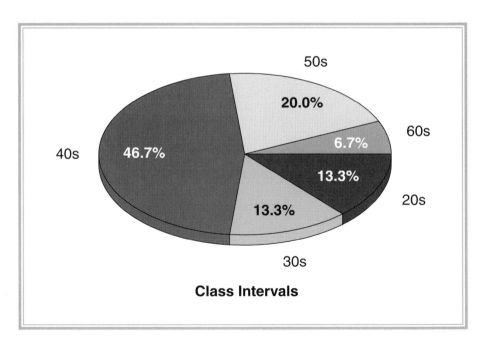

Figure 5: The pie chart indicates the percentages of years from 1920 to 1934 in which the annual number of Babe Ruth's home runs fell into each category.

Table 17: Converting Raw Scores to Percentages

Raw Scores	Percentages	Degrees
20s: 2	2/15 = 13.3%	.133 x 360 = 47.88°
30s: 2	2/15 = 13.3%	.133 x 360 = 47.88°
40s: 7	7/15 = 46.7%	.467 x 360 = 168.12°
50s: 3	3/15 = 20.0%	.200 x 360 = 72.00°
60s: 1	1/15 = 6.7%	.067 x 360 = 24.12°
$n = 15$	Total: 100%	Total: 360°

To construct a pie chart:

1. Change the frequency of each category to a percentage.

2. Multiply each percentage by 360 (the number of degrees in a circle) to obtain the number of degrees to assign to each component.

3. Use a protractor to mark off each component on the pie chart.

4. Label each segment with the corresponding percentage of the total.

Chapter 3

Descriptive Statistics

An *average* is a way of representing a set of data with a single descriptive number. It is one of many descriptive statistics. But the term average can be very deceptive. For instance, what is the average of the following five science test scores?

$$100, 100, 80, 40, 30$$

You might be inclined to say that the average is 70. However, another person could look at the same set of data and state that the average score is 80, since 80 is the middle score. And yet a third could say it is 100, since it occurs most frequently. And they would all be right! How could that be? It has to do with different measures of central tendency. They are called the *mean*, the *median*, and the *mode*.

When most people say "average," they are referring to the mean. The mean is the total sum of the numbers divided by the quantity of the numbers. For the science test scores, you would add all five scores for a sum of 350. Then you would divide the sum, 350, by the number of scores, 5, for an average of 70:

$$\frac{100 + 100 + 80 + 40 + 30}{5} = \frac{350}{5} = 70$$

The formula for the mean is

$$\bar{x} = \frac{\sum x}{n},$$

where $\sum$ is a mathematical symbol meaning "sum," x represents the data, and n is the number of data values. The symbol for the mean is $\bar{x}$, pronounced "x bar."

The mean is very sensitive to a single extreme score. If the lowest science test score of 30 were replaced with a score of 0, then you would have the following:

100, 100, 80, 40, 0

The mean would become 64, a drop of 6 points! A single very high score similarly affects the mean.

The median is the number found in the middle position of a list of values. For the science test scores, the median is 80 because it is the score in the middle of the list. When you have many pieces of data, arrange them in order, then assign each one a position, as follows:

Positions: (1)   (2)   (3)   (4)   (5)
Scores: 100 100   80   40   30

The position numbers help you find the middle score. When there are an odd number of scores, the middle position number is always the middle position number. In this case, 3 is the middle position number. Therefore the median is 80.

Finding the median for an even number of scores is not so straightforward. You must calculate the arithmetic mean of the two middle scores. Suppose you have the following six scores:

Positions:	(1)	(2)	(3)	(4)	(5)	(6)
Scores:	100	100	80	70	40	30

The median is the mean of the two middle scores, which are in positions 3 and 4. Therefore the median is 75.

The median is a good average to use when there is a single extreme or indeterminate score. For instance, suppose your experiment involved timing mice as they ran through a maze. After you had timed five mice, the sixth mouse refused to run the maze. To find the average running time, you should include all the scores. But if you include the sixth mouse's time as 0, it will throw your average running time off. The median will give you a pretty accurate average running time, even with the aberrant piece of data. The median allows you to exclude the sixth mouse, since it is a missing data point. (A missing data point is a data value not completed during the experiment.) The median will give you the "average" for the five mice that actually ran.

The mode is the value or score that appears the most often in a list of data. The value 100 appears twice in the list of science scores, and the values 80, 40, and 30 appear only once. The number 100 is the mode of the five test scores because it appears most often. The mode is appropriate for projects in which it is important to find the most common value in a distribution. Although it is not true for this example, the mode can also give a quick rough estimate of central tendency.

Sometimes two values appear in a list of scores the exact same number of times. If each occurs more often than any other value, then you have a *bimodal* distribution. And if more than two values appear most often in your list the same number of times, you have a *multimodal* distribution.

The mode is easy to compute, but as you have seen, it can be very far off from what most people consider average.

Percentiles

A data value by itself is meaningless. It takes on meaning only when it is compared with the rest of the values in the data set.

Suppose your sister announced, "I got 156 on my chemistry aptitude test." What would your reaction be? Would you commend her for a fine score or would you criticize her for not getting a higher score? Or would you reserve judgment until you learned more about the scores of the other students in your sister's class or the highest possible score? Of course, that would be the wisest course.

If your sister told you, "Eighty-seven percent of the students scored the same or lower than I did," she would be providing a frame of reference for interpreting the score. Indeed, she would have been telling you the *percentile rank* of her score.

The percentile rank of a given score is the percent of scores in a tested population, or group, that are equal to or lower than the given score. So if your sister said her score of 156 had a percentile rank of 87, she would be saying that 87 percent of her classmates scored 156 or lower on the chemistry aptitude test. With this information, you would know immediately that she did very well.

The most obvious way to calculate percentile rankings is to rank the scores in increasing order, and then calculate the percentage of scores at or below a given score.

Examine, for instance, the following list of ten chemistry grades ranked in increasing order:

Rank: (1) (2) (3) (4) (5) (6) (7) (8) (9) (10)
Score: 68 76 77 80 80 80 85 88 90 94

If you wanted to calculate the percentile rank of the score 77, you would note that there are 3 scores less than or equal to 77. Three scores out of ten scores translates to a percentage

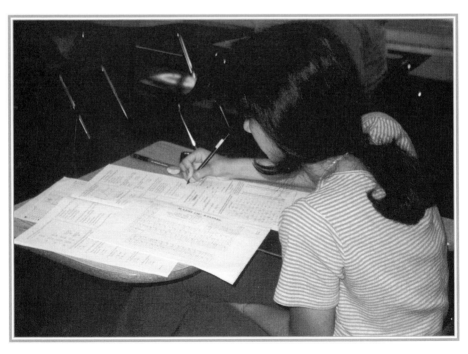

If your sister said she scored in the 87th percentile on a chemistry test, how well did she do?

Table 18. Cumulative Frequency Distribution for the Ten Science Scores

Score	f	cum f
94	1	10
90	1	9
88	1	8
85	1	7
80	3	6
77	1	3
76	1	2
68	1	1

of 30. The percentile rank of the score 77 is 30 percent; in other words, 30 percent of the grades are at or below 77.

The percentile rank can also be determined directly from a cumulative frequency table. Table 18 displays the cumulative frequency distribution of the ten chemistry grades.

If you wanted to know the percentile rank of the score 80, you could simply look up its cumulative frequency in the table. A cumulative frequency of 6 means that 6 out of 10, or 60 percent, of the grades are at or below 80. You can use the following equation to calculate percentile rank if you know the cumulative frequency:

$$\text{Percentile Rank} = \frac{cum\ f}{n} \times 100$$

where n is the total number of scores, or data values.

The calculation of percentile rank for the score of 90 is as follows:

$$\text{Percentile Rank} = \frac{cum\ f}{n} \times 100$$

$$\text{P. R.} = \frac{9}{10} \times 100$$

$$= 90\ \%$$

Special Percentiles

For convenience, percentiles are sometimes divided into sub-sets. *Deciles*, for example, break percentiles into 10 groups of 10 percentage points each. The first decile is equivalent to the 10th percentile, and the ninth decile is equal to the 90th percentile. Schools often give the scores for standardized tests of mathematics and reading in the form of deciles. SAT I test scores include deciles.

Quartiles break up the range of percentiles into fourths. The first quartile, Q_1, is the 25th percentile; the second quartile, Q_2, is the 50th percentile; and the third quartile, Q_3, is the 75th percentile. Note that the second quartile, Q_2, is the median of the data.

Suppose you wanted to find the quartiles for the following set of golf scores from 11 members of the high school golf team participating in match play:

89, 90, 87, 95, 86, 81, 102, 105, 83, 88, 91

First, rank the data from smallest to largest:

(1)	(2)	(3)	(4)	(5)	(6)	(7)	(8)	(9)	(10)	(11)
81	83	86	87	88	89	90	91	95	102	105

Then find the median by choosing the middle position—in this case position 6. This defines the second quartile, so Q_2 is 89. To find the first quartile, find the median of the lower half of the data. This includes only the data that is less than the median, as follows:

(1) (2) (3) (4) (5)
81   83   86   87   88

The median for these scores is position 3. Thus, the first quartile score is 86.

Now find the median of the upper half of the data to get the third quartile. The upper half of the data is:

(7) (8) (9) (10) (11)
90   91   95   102   105

The median for these scores is position 9. Thus, the third quartile score is 95.

To summarize, the quartile values for the golf scores are:

$$Q_1: 86 \quad Q_2: 89 \quad Q_3: 95$$

There are many ways to calculate quartiles, but a common general rule is:

1. Rank the data from smallest to largest.

2. Find the median. This is the second quartile, Q_2.

3. Find the median of the lower half of the data. This will be the first quartile, Q_1.

4. Find the median of the upper half of the data. This will be the third quartile, Q_3.

Five-Number Summaries and Boxplots

It is often convenient to include the minimum and maximum values with the quartiles to quickly summarize a distribution. This is called a *five-number summary*. The five-number summary of the golf scores is:

81, 86, 89, 95, 105

81: the smallest (minimum)

86: first quartile

89: second quartile

95: third quartile

105: the largest (maximum)

Note that the numbers are given in increasing order, so that you can see at a glance the spread and shape of the data. You can tell that most of the scores are concentrated in the 80s, with the best score at 81, and the worst score at 105. Remember that in golf the goal is to score low.

Let's find the five-number summary of another set of data. Suppose a marketing consultant wanted to get an idea of how much shoppers spent at a grocery store. She observes 11 shoppers at the store's checkout lanes and records their expenditures, rounded to the nearest dollar, in increasing order as follows:

A survey of a random sample of grocery shoppers can indicate their spending patterns.

(1)	(2)	(3)	(4)	(5)	(6)	(7)	(8)	(9)	(10)	(11)
2	10	11	12	15	18	20	24	27	43	64

Minimum spent: 2

First quartile Q_1: 11

Second quartile Q_2: 18

Third quartile Q_3: 27

Maximum spent: 64

Thus the five-number summary is: 2, 11, 18, 27, 64. It gives a quick overview of the grocery spending patterns of the marketing consultant's random sample of customers.

You can absorb the information of the five-number summary more easily if you put it in a *boxplot*, which is essentially a pictorial representation of the summary. The boxplot for the golf scores from the high school golf team is drawn in Figure 6. The values from the five-number summary are plotted on a vertical scale, and a box is drawn from Q_1 to Q_3 to emphasize where most of the data is found.

Notice that a horizontal line is drawn through the box at Q_2, the median, and that vertical lines extend from the box to the minimum and maximum values. These vertical lines are known as *whiskers*. The box shows you where most of the spending is concentrated, and the whiskers show the extremes of the data. This gives you an idea of the shape of the distribution in much the same way a stem-and-leaf diagram does. But unlike a stem-and-leaf diagram, a boxplot can display very large sets of data.

To make a boxplot summary:

1. Draw a vertical scale that includes your range of data.

2. To the right of the scale, draw a box from Q_1 to Q_3.

Figure 6: This boxplot shows that most grocery shoppers spent between $11 and $27 and that the average spent was $18.

3. Draw a horizontal line through the box at Q_2.

4. Draw lines, or whiskers, from Q_1 to the lowest value and from Q_3 to the highest value.

Dispersion: The Spread of the Scores

An average is a very important statistic, one that scientists invariably rely on in analyzing data. It is very powerful because it can summarize a set of data with just one number. But without other statistics, an average can sometimes be misleading.

To see this for yourself, imagine that you have a friend, Ellen, who has a craving for chocolate candy bars with nuts. You want to surprise her for her birthday with a whole case of candy bars. But Ellen is very particular; she likes exactly 40 nuts in each bar.

Table 19. Average Number of Nuts Per Candy Bar

Company	Mean nuts per bar
X	40
Y	40
Z	39.5

Which brand should you buy to guarantee that she is satisfied? You have three brands to choose from: X, Y, and Z. You decide to write the companies and question them about the average number of nuts in each bar.

Each company writes back with the requested information, along with a complimentary random sample of six of its candy bars. The information the companies provided on the mean number of nuts for each of the candy bars is summarized in Table 19.

The information looks very promising, but just to make sure the information is accurate, you decide to test the candy

Table 20. Number of Nuts in a Random Sample of Company X Candy Bars

Candy Bar	Number of Nuts
1	79
2	1
3	1
4	79
5	79
6	1

How many nuts are in each candy bar?

samples. You want to be certain Ellen will receive 40 nuts in each of the chocolate bars.

First, you test a bar from Company X. To your amazement, you discover 79 nuts in the first bar! So you test the remaining bars from Company X and obtain the results in Table 20.

Clearly, you cannot rely on Company X for 40 nuts per bar! You go on to test the samples from Company Y and obtain the results in Table 21.

These results are better than those for Company X, but they still will not satisfy Ellen. So on to Company Z. Initially, this brand seemed the least promising of the three because the mean number of nuts per candy bar is 39.5, rather than 40. But as you can see in Table 22, the number of nuts in each of the Z chocolate bars is quite consistent, either 39 or

Table 21. Number of Nuts in a Random Sample of Company Y Candy Bars

Candy Bar	Number of Nuts
1	50
2	30
3	45
4	35
5	43
6	37

40 nuts per bar. The choice for Ellen's gift is quite clear: Brand Z.

Why were the means for brands X and Y so misleading? The mean gives you information only about the center of each distribution; it does not tell you about the spread of the data around the center, and it gives no indication as to the consistency of the data.

So an average taken by itself may not always be very meaningful. To completely understand the results of your experiments, you need a statistic describing the spread of the data.

There are several different ways to measure the spread of data. The three most common statistics for the spread are the *range*, the *interquartile range*, and the *standard deviation*.

The range, sometimes called the crude range, is simply the difference between the maximum and minimum scores in your set of data:

range = maximum − minimum

The range for each of the candy companies is shown in Table 23.

Using Statistics in Science Projects, Internet Enhanced

Table 22. Number of Nuts in a Random Sample of Company Z Candy Bars

Candy Bar	Number of Nuts
1	40
2	40
3	40
4	39
5	39
6	39

The smaller the range, the smaller the spread of the scores. When the range is 0, there is no deviation or spread of scores around the mean. All the scores are exactly the same.

Unfortunately, the range gives no indication of whether the maximum or minimum value is an outlier or a score that is representative of your collected data. Furthermore, the range does not tell you if there is only 1 score or 20 scores at the maximum or minimum value.

For this reason, the range is not the best estimate of the spread of data, but it is a good quick estimate.

The interquartile range is more meaningful than the crude range. This statistic, commonly called the IQR, eliminates the

Table 23. Range of Nuts Found in a Random Sample of Candy Bars from Brands X, Y, And Z

Company	Maximum — Minimum	Range
X	79–1	78
Y	50–30	20
Z	40–39	1

54

data at the extremes, so that it is not affected by outliers. It is the range of the half of the data at the center of the distribution. The IQR begins at the 25th percentile and ends at the 75th percentile.

Thus, the data points are broken into quarters, and the points at each division are called quartiles. The first quartile, Q_1, is the data point at the 25th percentile. The second quartile, Q_2, is the data point at the 50th percentile and is also known as the median. The third quartile, Q_3, is the data point at the 75th percentile.

Let's calculate the IQR for the 11 golf scores discussed previously:

$$81, 83, 86, 87, 88, 89, 90, 91, 95, 102, 105$$

The crude range is $105 - 81 = 24$. The total spread of the scores is 24 points. The quartiles for this group of data are as follows:

$$Q_1: 86 \quad Q_2: 89 \quad Q_3: 95$$

The IQR is calculated as follows:

$$IQR = Q_3 - Q_1$$
$$= 95 - 86$$
$$= 9$$

Thus, the middle half of the data has a spread of 9 points. There is a difference of only 9 points between the scores for the half of the team at the center of the distribution, whereas there is a difference of 24 points between the best and worst player. This indicates that the data clusters around the median.

The standard deviation is the most commonly used statistic for indicating the spread of data points. It gives a precise measure of how the scores are spread around the center, or the mean, of your data. The standard deviation takes into account the values of all the points rather than just a few key ones, as the IQR does. The following formula defines the standard deviation, where, $\bar{x}$ is the mean, and n is the number of data points.

$$s = \sqrt{\frac{\Sigma (x - \bar{x})^2}{n-1}}$$

Let's compute the standard deviation for Brand Z, using the above formula. The values of x can be obtained from Table 22. The value of n is 6 and the value of $\bar{x}$ is 39.5. Substituting the values:

$$s = \sqrt{\frac{(40 - 39.5)^2 + (40 - 39.5)^2 + (40 - 39.5)^2 + (39 - 39.5)^2 + (39 - 39.5)^2 + (39 - 39.5)^2}{5}}$$

$$s = \sqrt{\frac{(0.5)^2 + (0.5)^2 + (0.5)^2 + (-0.5)^2 + (-0.5)^2 + (-0.5)^2}{5}}$$

$$s = \sqrt{\frac{1.5}{5}}$$

$$s = \sqrt{0.3}$$

$$s = 0.55$$

Table 24 gives the standard deviation of the number of nuts for each of the three brands of candy bars.

The lower the standard deviation, the less the data varies from the mean. As expected, Brand Z is the most consistent in the number of nuts each bar contains. It has a standard

Table 24. Standard Deviations for Three Brands of Candy Bars

Brand	Standard Deviation
X	42.72
Y	7.32
Z	0.55

deviation of 0.55, which means that the number of nuts in each candy bar is almost exactly the same.

Brands X and Y have much larger standard deviations, indicating that the number of nuts in each bar varies a great deal. So the larger the value, the greater the spread of the scores around the mean, and the greater the range. A set of values that is totally consistent has a standard deviation of 0.

Chapter 4

The Normal Distribution

You are probably familiar with the expression "the teacher grades on a curve." You may know that in general, bell-curve grading is a good thing for students taking hard courses. With a bell curve, even if you get poor scores, you may end up with a good grade if you did better than most of the other students.

Now that you know a little about statistics, you can get a better understanding of just what grading on a bell curve is. The bell curve refers to the shape of the frequency distribution of grades. If you graph the number of As, Bs, Cs, Ds, and Fs given by a teacher who grades on the bell curve, you would get a something that looks like a bell, as shown in Figure 7.

There are just a few As and Fs at the edges of the bell, but as you go toward the middle, the number of Bs and Ds is higher, and the number of Cs is the highest. The number of Cs coincides with both the median and mean

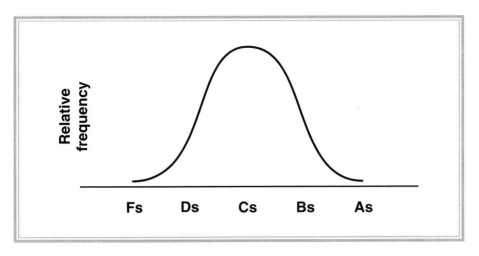

Figure 7. A graph of the normal distribution

of the grades. Grades usually do not follow this ideal shape, but teachers who grade on a bell curve will adjust them to conform to it. Statisticians call this shape a *normal distribution.* Many large sets of data naturally follow a normal distribution.

Let's look at one example. The owner of Steve's Skaterama was interested in buying new skates for his female customers, but he did not know how many of each size to order. So he surveyed the shoe sizes of his 340 female customers. He then used the results from his survey to create the frequency distribution in Table 25.

From this data, Steve concluded that the average shoe size for his population was 8 with a standard deviation of 1.73. Since the skates come only in whole sizes, these two statistics tell Steve that most of the females wear sizes from 6 to10. When Steve plotted the data, he obtained the frequency polygon in Figure 8.

Table 25. Frequency Distribution of Shoe Sizes of the 340 Female Customers at Steve's Skaterama

Size	f	Relative Frequency
4	5	5/340
5	25	25/340
6	35	35/340
7	65	65/340
8	80	80/340
9	65	65/340
10	35	35/340
11	25	25/340
12	5	5/340

He noticed that the curve was somewhat bell-shaped, had a single peak at the mean of 8, and seemed to be symmetric. In other words, it resembled a normal distribution.

To determine whether a distribution is truly normal, statisticians use a complex formula that includes the mean and standard deviation for a population. This formula can be found in any college-level statistics textbook. For the purposes of this book, we will examine the characteristics of the normal distribution, which are important for carrying out hypothesis testing in later chapters.

In every normal distribution, both the mean and the median are located in the center of the curve, or the top of the bell. In order to simplify calculations, statisticians have created a *standard normal curve* in which the mean is given a value of zero. Values to the left side of the mean are negative and the values to the right are positive, as in Figure 9. Thus, the values are symmetric around the mean.

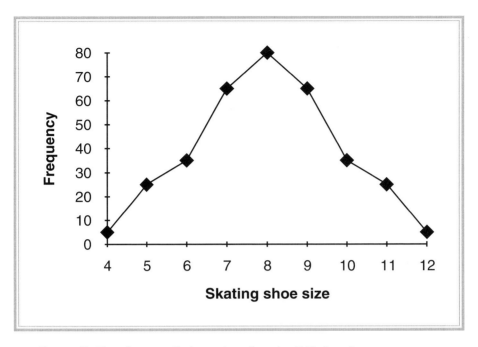

Figure 8: Distribution of shoe sizes for the 340 female customers at Steve's Skaterama

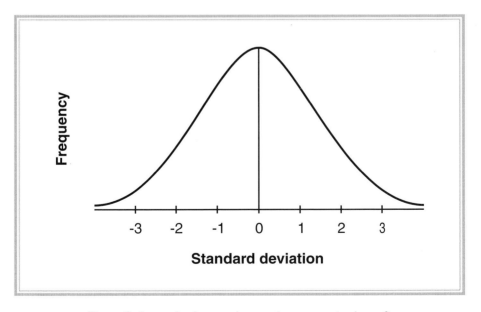

Figure 9: A standard normal curve is symmetric about 0.

What is more, the values along the horizontal axis of a standard normal curve correspond to units of standard deviation. As you recall from Chapter 3, the standard deviation is a measure of a curve's spread. In the standard normal curve, the standard deviation is given a value of 1.0.

For a normal distribution, statisticians have determined that:

- Approximately 68 percent of the data values fall within one standard deviation of the mean.

- Approximately 95 percent of the data values fall within two standard deviations of the mean.

- Approximately 99 percent of the data values fall within three standard deviations of the mean.

These ideas may become clearer if you look at Figure 10.

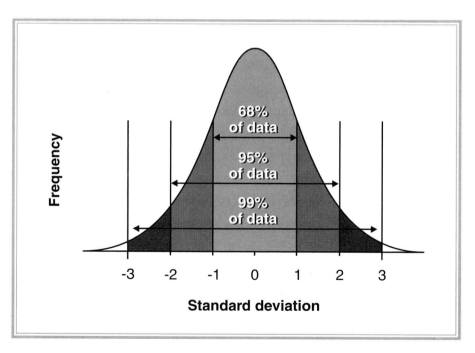

Figure 10: In the standard normal curve, the standard deviations marked off on the x-axis reveal the 68-95-99 properties of the normal distribution.

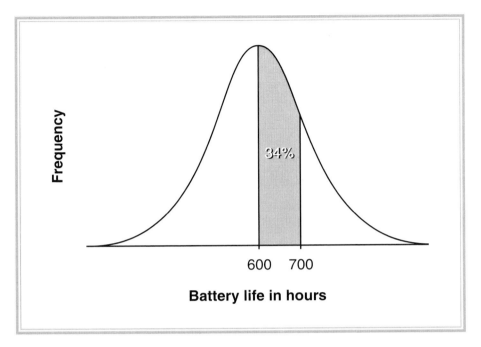

Figure 11: The number of hours a random sample of Dependable Batteries products lasted produced a normal distribution.

Statisticians work frequently with normal distributions because many real world applications seem to fall naturally into the shape of a normal distribution. The properties of the normal distribution allow them to make reliable predictions about the entire population from a small sample. For example, normal distributions can give the *probability* that a piece of data from a population falls within a certain range of values. This will become clearer by looking at a specific case.

Battery manufacturers are always working to increase the life of their batteries because customers want batteries that will last as long as possible. One manufacturer, Dependable Batteries, ran tests on a random sample of its products and found that the life of the batteries seemed to follow a normal distribution; the lifetimes were distributed along a bell curve, with a mean of 600 hours at the peak, as shown in Figure 11. If the standard deviation was 100 hours, what is the probability that a battery selected at random will last from 600 to 700 hours?

Since 700 is one standard deviation away from the mean, you know immediately that 34 percent of the batteries have lifetimes from 600 to 700 hours. Refer again to Figure 11 to verify this. Thus, there is a 34 percent chance that any battery picked at random from the assembly line will have a lifetime of 600 to 700 hours. Since a percentage of 100 gives a probability of 1.00, a percentage of 34 could be restated as a probability of 0.34.

Chapter 5

Correlation

Correlation describes the relationship between two variables. A statistic called the *correlation coefficient* indicates the strength of the relationship between two sets of data on a scale of −1 to 0 to 1, with 0 signifying that there is no relationship.

The correlation coefficient is different from the statistics you have studied so far because it describes the relationship between two variables rather than a single set of data.

Let's look at a situation in which the correlation coefficient would be useful. Suppose you are interested in determining whether there is a relationship between midterm grades and final exam scores. In other words, you want to know whether students with good midterm grades scored well on their final exams, and whether those with poor midterm grades scored poorly on their finals. You select three different science classes to study and choose a random sample of students from each class. The sample from the first class has the following grades:

Science Class I										
Student:	(1)	(2)	(3)	(4)	(5)	(6)	(7)	(8)	(9)	(10)
Midterm scores:	23	34	45	49	67	74	79	85	91	98
Final exam scores:	35	43	55	57	71	82	86	91	94	95

Notice that there is a pair of scores for each of the ten students. If the midterm score for each student is plotted along the x-axis, and the final score along the y-axis, a relationship between the two types of grades may become apparent. Indeed, as shown in Figure 12, the graph reveals a linear relationship between the *x* and *y* values; the points approximate a straight line.

Since low values of *x* are paired with low values of *y* and high values of *x* are paired with high values of *y*, the relationship is positive.

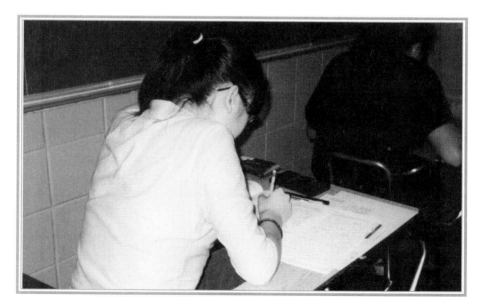

Is there a correlation between students' midterm grades and their final exam scores?

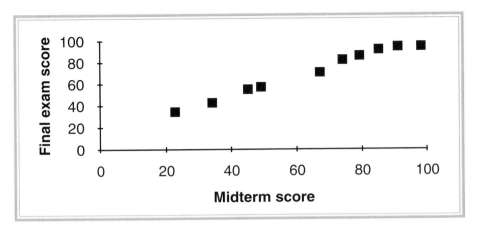

Figure 12: The exam scores for the first science class have a positive correlation.

The second science class had the following scores:

Science Class II										
Student:	(1)	(2)	(3)	(4)	(5)	(6)	(7)	(8)	(9)	(10)
Midterm scores:	96	90	87	84	80	73	68	65	64	53
Final exam scores:	40	55	60	59	67	70	77	78	85	90

When these scores are plotted, as in Figure 13, you can see an inverse, or negative, linear relationship between x and y variables. Students with high midterm grades had low final grades and those with low midterm grades had high final grades.

The scores from the third science class are as follows:

Science Class III										
Student:	(1)	(2)	(3)	(4)	(5)	(6)	(7)	(8)	(9)	(10)
Midterm scores:	23	75	35	64	94	86	45	54	46	99
Final exam scores:	76	89	45	90	54	38	98	27	67	34

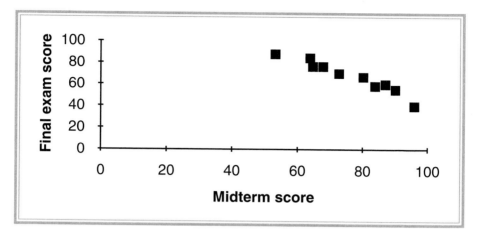

Figure 13: The exam scores for the second science class have a negative correlation.

The graph of the data is shown in Figure 14. It is obvious that there is little or no linear correlation between *x* and *y* because the points seem to be scattered randomly.

Figures 12, 13, and 14 are called scatter diagrams because they let you see how the data values are scattered. This scatter is a measure of the correlation between the *x* and *y* values.

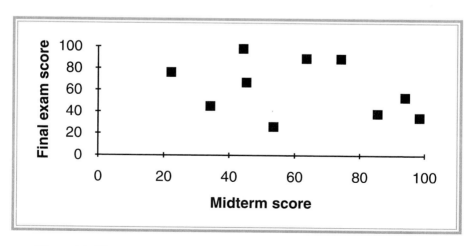

Figure 14: The exam scores for the third science class have no correlation.

Thus, scatter diagrams give a picture of the value of the correlation coefficient.

The basic scatter diagram portrays the direction, form, and strength of any relationship between two variables. But it is not always easy to guess the degree of the relationship from a visual inspection of a scatter diagram. The interpretation of a scatter diagram is surprisingly subjective. Stretching or compressing the graph, for instance, can dramatically alter its appearance.

Fortunately, rather than relying solely on a scatter plot, you can calculate a value for the correlation. The correlation coefficient, r, is a value between -1 and 1. If there is no correlation at all, the value of r is 0. Figure 15 shows how a scatter diagram for $r = 0$ might look.

If $r = 1$ or $r = -1$, then there is a perfect linear relationship between x and y values. All the graphed points would lie on a straight line. Figure 16 shows the scatter diagram for these cases.

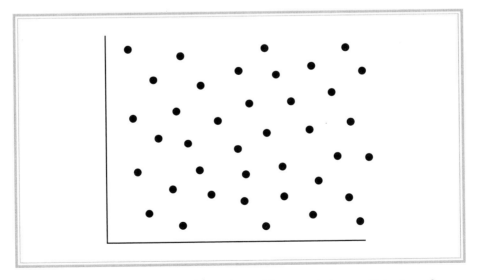

Figure 15: This scatter plot shows data with a correlation coefficient $r = 0$.

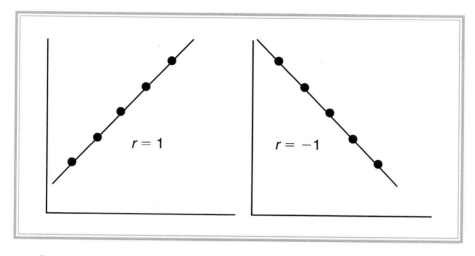

Figure 16: These scatter plots indicate correlation coefficients of $r = 1$ or $r = -1$.

If r is between 0 and 1, then the x and y values have a positive correlation, as shown in Figure 17.

If r is between -1 and 0, then the x and y values have a negative correlation, as shown in Figure 18.

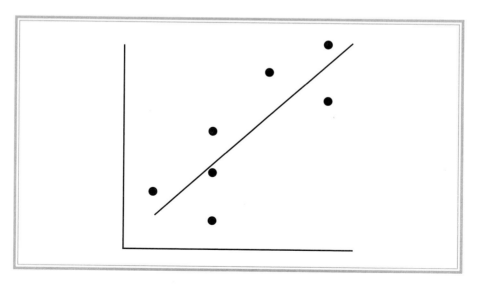

Figure 17: This scatter plot shows data when $0 < r < 1$.

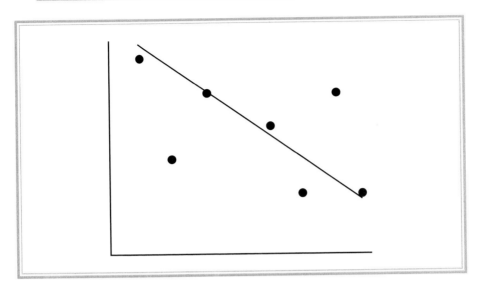

Figure 18: This scatter plot shows data with $-1 < r < 0$.

The sign of the correlation coefficient indicates the direction of the relationship. So both $r = -0.07$ and $r = +0.07$ indicate a relationship of exactly the same strength but in opposite directions. The formula for calculating the linear correlation coefficient is called the *Pearson r correlation coefficient formula*. This formula may look overwhelming at first, but you will find that it is relatively simple to use. And, of course, you can use a calculator or a computer program to simplify your task. Before calculating r, it is always a good idea to first draw a scatter diagram to get a rough idea of the correlation.

$$r = \frac{\sum xy - \frac{1}{n} \sum x \sum y}{\sqrt{(\sum x^2 - \frac{(\sum x)^2}{n})(\sum y^2 - \frac{(\sum y)^2}{n})}}$$

Let's look at the correlation between a child's height and age. The growth chart of Isabelle between the ages of 3 and 5 1/2 years is as follows:

Age in years:	3.0	3.5	4.0	4.5	5.0	5.5
Height in feet:	2.9	3.1	3.2	3.4	3.4	3.5

First make a scatter diagram to determine whether the correlation seems positive, negative, or close to zero. Plot age along the x-axis and height along the y-axis, as shown in Figure 19.

You should be able to easily see that the correlation is positive. Now to calculate r, you must first find the sums x (Σx), y (Σy), x^2 (Σx^2), y^2 (Σy^2) and xy (Σxy). You can obtain the values for $(\Sigma x)^2$ and $(\Sigma y)^2$ from Σx and Σy. The easiest way to determine all of these values is to create Table 26.

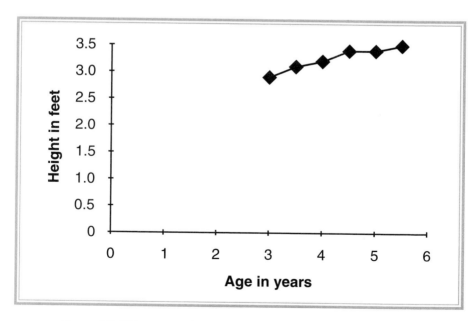

Figure 19: This scatter diagram shows Isabelle's growth with age.

Table 26. Sums (Σ) Necessary to Calculate the Pearson r Correlation Coefficient for Isabelle's Growth and Height

x(age)	y(height)	x^2	y^2	xy
3.0	2.9	9.0	8.41	8.70
3.5	3.1	12.25	9.61	10.85
4.0	3.2	16.00	10.24	12.80
4.5	3.4	20.25	11.56	15.30
5.0	3.4	25.00	11.56	17.00
5.5	3.5	30.25	12.25	19.25
Sum (Σ): 25.5	19.5	112.75	63.63	83.90

From the table, you can see that:

$\Sigma x = 25.5$

$\Sigma y = 19.5$

$\Sigma x^2 = 112.75$

$\Sigma y^2 = 63.63$

$\Sigma xy = 83.90$

$(\Sigma x)^2 = 650.25$

$(\Sigma y)^2 = 380.25$

Next, substitute these values in the Pearson r correlation coefficient formula:

$$r = \frac{\Sigma xy - \dfrac{1}{n} \Sigma x \, \Sigma y}{\sqrt{(\Sigma x^2 - \dfrac{(\Sigma x)^2}{n})(\Sigma y^2 - \dfrac{(\Sigma y)^2}{n})}}$$

$$r = \frac{(83.90) - (\frac{1}{6})(25.5)(19.5)}{\sqrt{(112.75 - \frac{650.25}{6})(63.63 - \frac{380.25}{6})}}$$

$$r = \frac{83.9 - 82.88}{\sqrt{(112.75 - 108.38)(63.63 - 63.38)}}$$

$$r = \frac{1.02}{\sqrt{(4.37)(.25)}}$$

$$r = \frac{1.02}{\sqrt{1.09}}$$

$$r = \frac{1.02}{1.04}$$

$$r = 0.98$$

A correlation coefficient of 0.98 means that there is a very high positive correlation between Isabelle's age and growth.

When using this formula, it is important to remember that the Pearson r correlation coefficient reflects only the *linear* relationship between two variables. If you calculate a low correlation coefficient, you cannot immediately conclude that there is little or no relationship between the two variables you are studying. They could be related in a nonlinear way. This is much more difficult to test for and beyond the scope of this book. Just remember that the failure to find a correlation means one of two things:

1. The variables are unrelated.

2. The variables are related in a nonlinear fashion.

If you do find a correlation, it is also important to avoid assuming that a change in one variable is causing a change in the other variable. A strong correlation does not necessarily imply cause and effect. Some other known or unknown variable could be causing changes in both variables.

Chapter 6

Inferential Statistics

The preceding chapters deal with statistics that apply to a sample taken from a population. In the real world, it is not enough to work with samples. Scientists must draw conclusions about the entire population based on what they learn from samples. In this chapter, you will learn techniques for making inferences about the population from samples.

To avoid confusion, statisticians identify the measurable characteristics, or statistics, of a sample with regular lowercase letters and the measurable characteristics of a population with lowercase Greek letters. For example, the symbol for the mean of a sample is $\bar{x}$, which is pronounced "x bar," whereas the symbol for the mean of the population is the Greek letter mu, or μ, which is pronounced "moo." The symbol for the standard deviation of a sample is s, and the symbol for the standard deviation of a population is the Greek letter sigma, or σ. The symbol for the correlation coefficient for a sample is r, whereas the symbol for the population correlation coefficient is the Greek letter rho, or ρ, pronounced "row."

Hypothesis Testing

If a statistician asks 100 people how they intend to vote in an upcoming election, his primary goal is not to determine exactly how these 100 people will vote, but to infer from this sample how the entire voting population will cast their ballots.

Hypothesis testing is a mathematical procedure for analyzing the statistics from a sample in order to make inferences about an entire population. As you learned in the introduction, a hypothesis is a guess, or conjecture, about a population parameter that you make before you begin an experiment. Whether you accept or reject the hypothesis will depend on the information you acquire from studying the sample.

Hypothesis testing is a statistical procedure that lets you decide to accept or reject your original hypothesis. This is accomplished by restating the original hypothesis in the form of two mutually exclusive hypotheses; the *null hypothesis* and the *alternative hypothesis*.

In a null hypothesis, the researcher proposes that there is no difference between the sample statistic and the population parameter. For instance, in the above example, the null hypothesis would be: There is no difference between the voting patterns of the sample of 100 people and the general population. The symbol for the null hypothesis is H_o. Mathematically, the null hypothesis always tests the sample statistic value against the population parameter; that is, $\bar{x}$, the value for the mean obtained from the sample, is tested against μ for the population, and r, the correlation coefficient for the sample, is tested against ρ for the population.

In an alternative hypothesis, the researcher proposes that there is a difference between the sample statistic and the population parameter. The symbol for the alternative hypothesis is H_1.

A statistician works with the null and alternative hypotheses at the same time.

Suppose you want to see if there is a difference between two manufacturing methods. First, you create the null hypothesis. You proclaim that there is no difference between the two manufacturing methods; that is, both methods give exactly the same results. Second, you create the alternative hypothesis. You proclaim that there is a difference between the two manufacturing methods; both methods do not give the same results. In other words, one manufacturing method is clearly different from the other.

The null hypothesis is created just to see if you can reject it. It might seem odd, but statisticians discuss the results of hypothesis testing only in terms of the null hypothesis; that is, they either reject or accept the null hypothesis. Statisticians never use the alternative hypothesis to discuss the results of hypothesis testing. In the example on the two manufacturing methods, if you discover that there is no difference between the two manufacturing methods, you would accept the null hypothesis. If you discover that there is a difference between the two manufacturing methods, you would reject the null hypothesis.

The Z-Test

For a more complex example, suppose a teacher gives her twelfth-grade class a final examination and the average score is 75. In other words, her sample of 36 students has a mean score of $\bar{x} = 75$. From her years of experience teaching the class, the teacher knows that the average score for all students who have taken the test is a μ of 68, with a standard deviation, or σ, of 6. She wants to know whether this year's class is really superior to previous classes, as the numbers seem to indicate.

It may seem obvious to you that this year's average is superior to the average from previous years. But if the test scores in the population varied quite a bit, a difference of 7 points in the average score may be insignificant from a statistical point of view. Hypothesis testing can be used to determine whether the 7-point difference between the sample mean of 75 and the population mean of 68 is meaningful, or *statistically significant.*

The null hypothesis, H_o, is stated as follows:

$$H_o: \mu = 68$$

This is a mathematical way of saying there is no difference between the population mean of 68 and the sample mean of 75. In other words, a group of 36 students who scored a mean of 75 could have come from the population of previous students.

The alternative hypothesis, H_1, is as follows:

$$H_1: \mu > 68$$

This is a mathematical way of saying there is a difference between the population mean of 68 and the sample mean of

75. In other words, a group of 36 students who scored a mean of 75 could not possibly have come from the population of previous students; they must be from a different superior population.

It is important to keep in mind that any decisions that you make based on samples always have the possibility of being in error. If you reject the null hypothesis when it is in fact true, you have made an error known as a *type I error*. On the other hand, if you accept the null hypothesis when it is in fact false, you have made an error known as a *type II error*. Table 27 outlines all possible outcomes of hypothesis testing.

The probability of a type I error in a test is called the *level of significance* and is denoted by the Greek letter alpha, or a. Researchers choose the level of significance before they have collected any data so as not to influence their results. It is a measure of the risk they are willing to take of getting a type I error. The lower you set the level of significance, the less the likelihood of a type I error, but the greater the likelihood of a type II error.

One of the most commonly used values for alpha is $a = 0.05$. This means that five times out of 100 you will reject the null hypothesis when the null hypothesis should actually be accepted.

Another commonly used value for alpha is $a = 0.01$. A 1% level of significance indicates that the null hypothesis

Table 27. Possible Outcomes of Hypothesis Testing

Decision	H_oTrue	H_oFalse
Reject H_o	Type I Error	Correct Decision; No Error
Accept H_o	Correct Decision; No Error	Type II Error

will be rejected when it should be accepted only once in 100 cases.

Let's return to the example in which this year's students obtained an average of 75 on the final exam. Suppose that the teacher has chosen a level of significance of 5 percent. The next step is to test the hypothesis.

Since you know both the mean and standard deviation for the population, the proper statistical test to use in this case is the z-test. The formula for the z-test is:

$$z = \frac{\bar{x} - \mu}{\dfrac{\sigma}{\sqrt{n}}}$$

The formula may seem complicated at first, but you have all the values needed to calculate *z*. You know:

- $\bar{x} = 75$; the sample mean—this year's final exam average—is 75.

- $\mu = 68$; the population mean—the average for all the previous years—is 68.

- $\sigma = 6$; the population standard deviation is 6.

- $n = 36$; the sample size—the number of students in the present class—is 36.

$$z = \frac{\bar{x} - \mu}{\dfrac{\sigma}{\sqrt{n}}}$$

Substituting these values into the z-test formula, you obtain:

$$z = \frac{75 - 68}{\frac{6}{\sqrt{36}}}$$

$$z = 7$$

You have calculated a value of $z = 7$, but what does this mean? Should you accept or reject your null hypothesis? In order to interpret z values, statisticians use a geometric model of the standard normal curve, which was explained in Chapter 4. Remember, the standard normal curve is symmetric, and has a value of 0 for the mean. The values along the horizontal axis of the normal curve correspond to z values.

The standard normal curve consists of a left tail, the center, and a right tail, as shown in Figure 20.

For the purposes of hypothesis testing, the area in the tails is known as the rejection region. The remaining area is known as the acceptance region. The value on the horizontal axis that separates the rejection region from the acceptance region is

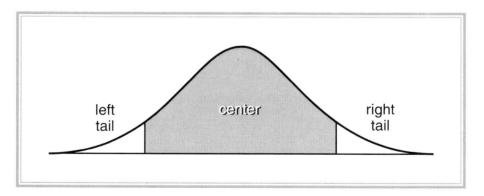

Figure 20: The standard normal curve is divided into three sections for hypothesis testing.

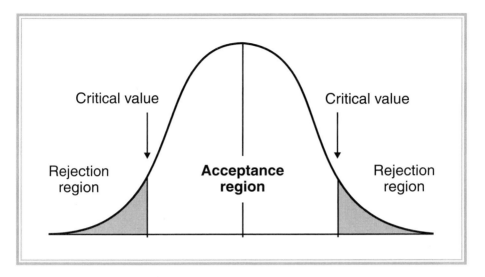

Critical value

Critical value

Rejection
region

**Acceptance
region**

Rejection
region

Figure 21: The test of the hypothesis involves finding the region the z value falls into.

known as the *critical value*. You will reject the null hypothesis if the *z* value falls in the rejection region and you will accept the null hypothesis if the *z* value falls in the acceptance region of the standard normal curve model. See Figure 21.

A list of critical values for different levels of significance (alpha, or α) can be found in Table I in Appendix C. For our example, the rejection region is only in the right tail since we want to know whether the population mean for this year's class is greater than the mean for previous classes. So we must look up the value for a *one-tailed test*. (Two-tailed tests will be explained later.) The critical value for this example, where $\alpha = 0.05$, is 1.65. This means that the value 1.65 will separate the rejection region from the acceptance region as shown in Figure 22.

Since the value that you obtained from the *z* formula, $z = 7.00$, is larger than 1.65, your *z* falls in the rejection region, as shown in Figure 23.

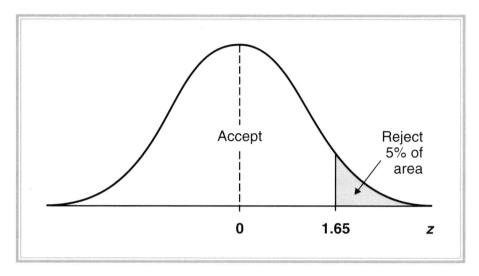

Figure 22: The critical value determines where the acceptance region ends and the rejection region begins.

Therefore, you reject the null hypothesis. That means you reject the idea that this class is from the same population as all previous classes that have taken the final exam.

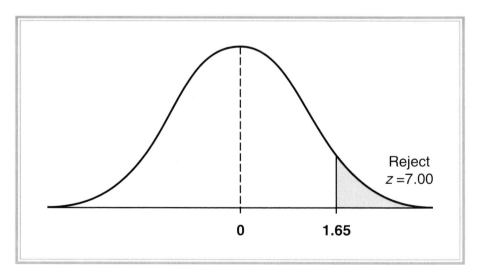

Figure 23: The z value clearly falls in the rejection region, so you must reject the null hypothesis.

Let There Be Light

The Superlight Light Bulb Company claims that its 100-watt bulb has an average life of μ = 1,000 hours with a standard deviation of σ = 75 hours. Suppose Elana wanted to confirm this by conducting an experiment on a random sample of 64 bulbs. After leaving the bulbs on until they burn out, she finds that the average bulb life for the sample is $\bar{x}$ = 975 hours. Has she caught the company in a lie? Is the real mean less than 1,000 hours?

The null hypothesis is:

$$H_o: \mu = 1,000$$

It says that there is no significant difference between the average bulb life of the sample and the average bulb life of the population, as specified by the company.

The alternative hypothesis is:

$$H_1: \mu < 1,000$$

It says that the average bulb life of the sample is less than the average bulb life of the population.

Let's assume that the Superlight Light Bulb Company has agreed to accept our findings, at an α = 0.01 level of significance. Since you know both the population mean and population standard deviation, you can use the z-test.

Before finding the z value, let's get the critical value from Table I in Appendix C. It is a good idea to first sketch your distribution with acceptance and rejection regions marked so that you do not get confused in the course of the z-test. Our geometric model of the problem is shown in Figure 24.

In Table I, you will find a z value of 2.33 for a 0.01 level of significance. You must add a negative sign to this value because

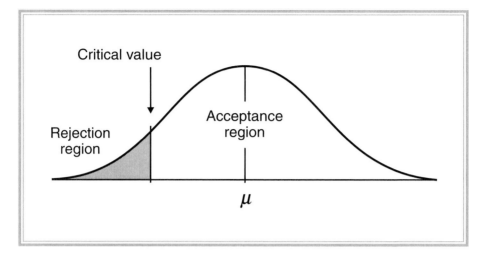

Figure 24: The rejection region is in the left tail because the life of your light bulbs is less than the company's average.

the average life of the sample bulbs ($\bar{x} = 975$) is less than the life of the population bulbs ($\mu = 1,000$). You want to know whether the population mean for this sample is actually less than 1,000 hours, so you must use the left tail, or negative tail, to test your null hypothesis. The z-test says to reject H_o if $z < -2.33$. You can now calculate the value of z for the light bulbs:

$$z = \frac{\bar{x} - \mu}{\dfrac{\sigma}{\sqrt{n}}}$$

$$z = \frac{1,000 - 975}{\dfrac{75}{\sqrt{64}}}$$

$$z = -2.67$$

Now you have all the information you need to draw a conclusion. The value of $z = -2.67$ falls in the rejection region. You must reject H_0 and conclude that the mean of the bulbs is not as the manufacturer states, but is less than 1,000 hours. Superlight will have to change its advertising claim.

In some cases, you will not know both the population mean and the population standard deviation. If you know the population mean, but not the population standard deviation, then you should use the t-test rather than the z-test. The next example illustrates how to use the t-test.

Sizing Up Fish With the T-Test

Tara owns a private fishing pond. She boasts that the average length of fish in the pond is 15 inches ($\mu = 15$). To see whether she is telling the truth, you catch a sample of 23 fish from various random locations in the pond. You find the average length of this sample of fish to have a sample mean of 10.7 ($\bar{x} = 10.7$) inches with a sample standard deviation, $s = 4.8$ inches. Given this data, can Tara's claim possibly be true? Could this sample have come from a population whose mean is 15, or are the fish shorter than she states? Find the answer using a level of significance of $\alpha = 0.01$.

The null hypothesis is:

$$H_o: \mu = 15$$

The alternative hypothesis is:

$$H_1: \mu < 15$$

The alternative hypothesis says that the average size of the fish in the pond is less than 15 inches. Here again, we must carry out a one-tailed test.

In this case, you cannot use the z-test because you do not know the population standard deviation. The t-test is a good test to use in this situation. The t-test requires that you know the sample mean, the sample standard deviation, and the population mean. The underlying distribution, known as the *student's t distribution* is suitable for relatively small samples. As the sample size increases to about 200, the *t* distribution approaches the shape of the normal distribution. As shown in Figure 25, the *t* distribution has thicker tails than the standard normal distribution.

Figure 25 shows that the shape of the student's *t* distribution depends on the sample size. The sample size determines the *degrees of freedom* of the *t* distribution. This parameter, represented by *df*, is equal to the sample size minus 1:

$$df = n - 1 = 23 - 1 = 22$$

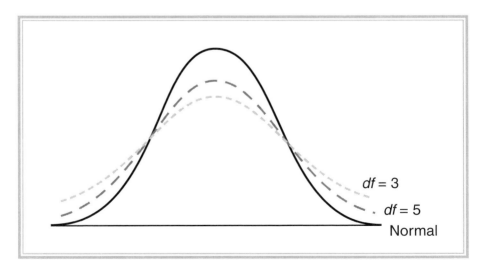

Figure 25: The shape of the student's t distribution depends on the number of degrees of freedom.

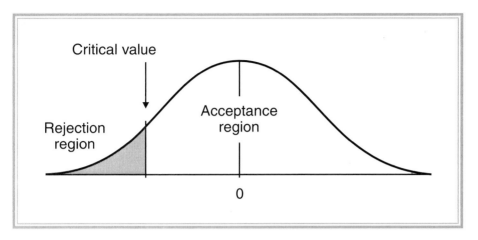

Figure 26: The rejection region of the *t* distribution is in the left tail because the fish you measured were shorter than Tara's claim.

There are 22 degrees of freedom in this sample.

You will be calculating a *t* value for your problem, just as you calculated a *z* value in the previous example. Before finding the *t* value, sketch your distribution, marking acceptance and rejection regions. As in the light bulb problem, the rejection region will be in the left tail since you want to know whether the mean is less than the stated value. The geometric model for this problem is shown in Figure 26.

Next, determine the critical value of *t* for this problem in Table II in Appendix C. Notice that Table II is quite different from Table I. In Table I, you need to know only the level of significance, but in Table II, you need to know α and the degrees of freedom for your problem.

For $\alpha = 0.01$ and 22 degrees of freedom, you should get a critical value of -2.51 from Table II. Notice that, as in the light bulb example, the value must be made negative. That is because you are testing whether the average length of the sample of fish is less than the average length of the population of fish. This means that you are using the left or negative tail to test your null hypothesis. So the t-test says to reject H_o if $t < -2.51$ as shown in Figure 27.

The formula for t is:

$$t = \frac{\bar{x} - \mu_0}{\frac{s}{\sqrt{n}}}$$

$$t = \frac{10.7 - 15}{\frac{4.8}{\sqrt{23}}} = -4.3$$

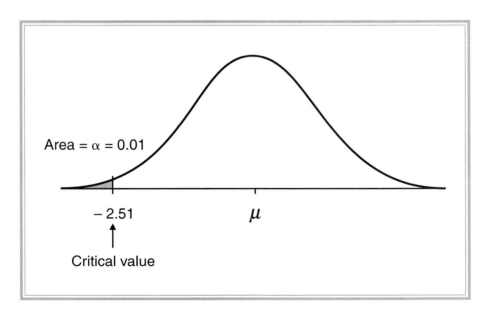

Figure 27: The rejection region for this t-test is very small because the level of significance is only 0.01.

Since $t = -4.3$ falls in the rejection region, you must reject the null hypothesis, and conclude that the fish are smaller than Tara claimed.

Tails of Two Regions

The examples you have worked on so far involve one rejection region located in one tail of the distribution. As a result, the hypothesis tests you performed are called one-tailed tests. A *two-tailed test* is necessary when the alternative hypothesis contains the not-equal sign ($\neq$), instead of a greater-than or less-than symbol (> or <).

Such a situation would occur, for instance, in the testing of jeans for consistency in size. A jeans manufacturer wants to make sure that the average waist measurement of its size-32 jeans be within a half inch of the labeled size. When a random sample of the jeans is inspected for quality, the manufacturer is interested only in whether the average size of the sample is significantly different from 32 inches. It does not matter whether the jeans are too big or too small; they will be rejected in either case. In this situation, the two hypotheses would be:

$$H_o: \mu = 32$$

$$H_1: \mu \neq 32$$

The geometric model for such a situation would look like Figure 28.

Thus, if the z or t value falls in either of the two tail regions, the null hypothesis must be rejected. Mathematically speaking, you would compare the absolute values of the test values as follows:

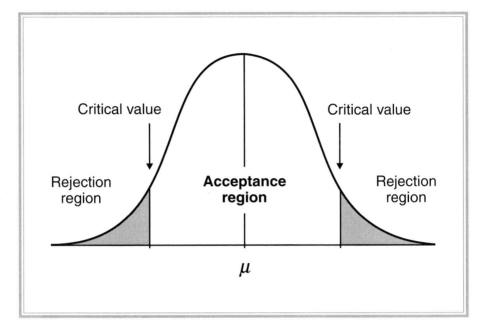

Figure 28: The geometric model for the case when the alternative hypothesis has a not-equal sign

Reject H_0 if |calculated z| > |z-test value|

The brackets, | |, designate absolute value, which is the value of a number excluding any negative sign.

It should be clear to you by now that the null hypothesis always contains an equal sign because you are testing that there is no significant difference between the sample mean ($\bar{x}$) and the population mean (μ). In making the hypothesis, you are assuming that the sample has come from the population. The alternative hypothesis, however, always contains one of three mathematical symbols: >, <, or ≠. As shown in Table 28, if the symbol is >, then the rejection region is in the right tail; if it is <, the rejection region is in the left tail; and if it is ≠, then the rejection region is in both tails.

Table 28. Determining Rejection Regions

If the symbol in the alternative hypothesis is:	One-Tail <	Two-Tail ≠	One-Tail >
then the critical or rejection region consists of:	one region on the left side	two regions, one on each side	one region on the right side

The ρ-Test

If your underlying distribution is the normal distribution and you want to test whether the correlation coefficient that you have obtained from your sample comes from a population in which the correlation coefficient is 0, you can apply the ρ-test. Remember from Chapter 5 that a correlation coefficient of 0 means that there is no relationship between the two variables.

For instance, suppose your friend Leo says that he thinks there is a strong correlation between the amount of natural gas used to heat his home and the number of degree-days for the 9 months shown in Table 29. (A degree-day is registered for every degree the temperature falls below 65° per day. Degree-days are used to measure weather severity.)

Table 29. Leo's Gas Usage from October to June

Month:	Oct.	Nov.	Dec.	Jan.	Feb.	Mar.	Apr.	May	June
Degree-days:	15.6	26.8	37.8	36.4	35.5	18.6	15.3	7.9	0
Gas usage:	5.2	6.1	8.7	8.5	8.8	4.9	4.5	2.5	1.1

Using the data found in Table 28, Leo found a sample correlation coefficient of $r = 0.989$, which is a very strong relationship.

You want to know whether Leo's finding was just a fluke or whether there is indeed a correlation between gas consumption and degree-days. In other words, is it possible that Leo's sample correlation could have come from a population in which the true correlation is zero?

This question leads to the following null hypothesis:

$$H_o: \rho = 0$$

In this null hypothesis, ρ is the correlation coefficient for the population from which this sample was drawn.

Since Leo expects gas consumption to be positively related to degree-days, it is appropriate to test the above null hypothesis against the following one-tailed alternative hypothesis:

$$H_1: \rho > 0$$

To test the null hypothesis, you must use the ρ-test, which is a special form of the t-test. The underlying distribution of the ρ-test is the student's t distribution. For the ρ-test, you must calculate the value for t using a different equation from the one used for the t-test. Use the following formula for t when you want to test whether a population correlation coefficient is 0 (i.e. $H_o: \rho = 0.00$):

$$t = \frac{r\sqrt{n-2}}{\sqrt{1-r^2}}$$

where n is the number of pairs of data values, which in our case is 9.

For the ρ-test, the number of degrees of freedom is the number of data values minus 2, as follows:

$$df = n - 2$$
$$df = 9 - 2$$
$$df = 7$$

Suppose you select a level of significance of 0.01. Now you can draw the geometric model for the test as shown in Figure 29.

Because the alternative hypothesis has a greater-than sign (>) in it, you have a one-tailed test with one rejection region as shown in Figure 29. Now you must determine the critical value using Table II in Appendix C. Looking in the row for $df = 7$, you should find a critical value of 3.0.

Calculating the t-test statistic you get:

$$t = \frac{.989 \sqrt{9-2}}{\sqrt{1 - .989^2}}$$

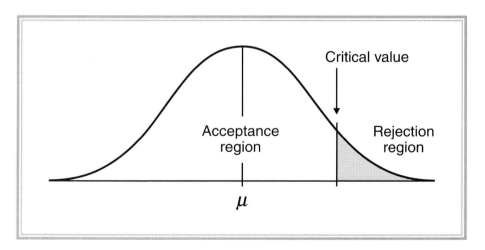

Figure 29: When testing for zero correlation between values, the rejection region is in the right tail.

$$t = \frac{2.6166}{.1479}$$

$$t = 17.69$$

Clearly, you can reject the null hypothesis, H_o, since 17.69 > 3.00. Now Leo has strong evidence that gas consumption is positively related to degree-days.

Other Tests

There are many tests other than the z-, t- and p-tests that can be used in hypothesis testing. Each one is designed for a specific type of distribution and set of circumstances. Now, let's look at examples using another of the more commonly used tests: the chi-square test. Chi is the Greek letter, χ, pronounced "ky."

Suppose that you are interested in the number of baseball games that were played in each of the World Series between 1922 and 1965. Since the first team to win four games wins the series, the World Series can last anywhere from four to seven games. The number of games played per series for the period 1922–1965 is shown in Table 30.

The series went to 4 games in 9 years, to 5 games in 8 years, and so on. The most frequently played number was 7 games, which happened in a whopping 18 years. The data

Table 30. Games in the World Series Between 1922 and 1965

Number of games in the World Series	4	5	6	7
Frequency of occurrence, or f_o, between 1922 and 1965	9	8	9	18

seems to indicate that it is more likely that 7 games will be played than any other number. But is this true? Or is it equally likely that any of the numbers of games will be played?

This is a different kind of statistical question from the previously discussed examples. Up until now, you have tested either the mean or the correlation coefficient value against the population value. However, in this example you are interested in comparing the distribution of data from sample years against a theoretical distribution in which each piece of data has the same probability of occurring. The chi-square test answers the following question: How well does the observed distribution fit the theoretical distribution?

The formula for the chi-square statistic is:

$$\chi^2 = \Sigma \frac{(f_o - f_e)^2}{f_e}$$

In this formula, f_o is the symbol for the actual, or observed, frequency count and f_e is the symbol for the expected frequency count.

The null hypothesis states that each event is equally likely to occur. This means that you expect the World Series to last for 4, 5, 6, or 7 games an equal number of times. This expected frequency can be calculated by finding the mean of the number of games played in each World Series from 1922 to 1965 as follows:

$$f_e = (9 + 8 + 9 + 18)/4$$

$$= 44/4$$

$$= 11$$

The null hypothesis states that each event is equally likely to occur. In other words, the World Series will last 4, 5, 6, or 7 games an equal number of times. Therefore:

$$H_o: f_e = 11$$

The alternative hypothesis states that each event is not equally likely to occur. In other words, the World Series will not last 4, 5, 6, or 7 games an equal number of times. Therefore:

$$H_1: f_e \neq 11$$

Let's test these hypotheses with a level of significance, $\alpha = 0.05$. The chi-square distribution is shown in Figure 30, with the rejection region marked. This is the geometric model for the problem.

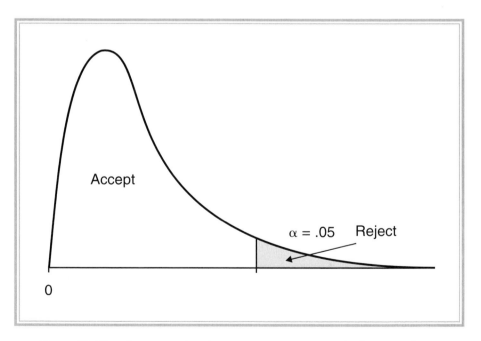

Figure 30: The chi-square distribution starts at zero on the horizontal axis and rises in the positive direction.

Notice that the chi-square values—the values along the horizontal axis—are always positive and that only one rejection region is possible, in the single tail of the distribution. For $\alpha = 0.05$, the rejection region makes up 5 percent of the area under the curve.

The shape of the chi-square distribution depends on the number of distinct values in the problem, or more specifically, the number of degrees of freedom, *df*. As in the t-test, *df* is equal to the number of different categories, *k*, minus 1. In this case:

$$df = k - 1$$

$$df = 4 - 1$$

$$df = 3$$

You can now look up the chi-square test value in Table III in Appendix C, which is set up in the same way as Table II for the *t* distributions. For an alpha value of 0.05, the critical value is 7.82. Thus, your test decision will be to reject the H_o if $x^2 \geq 7.82$.

Now you can calculate the chi-square value for this problem:

$$x^2 = \Sigma \frac{(9-11)^2}{11} + \frac{(8-11)^2}{11} + \frac{(9-11)^2}{11} + \frac{(18-11)^2}{11}$$

$$x^2 = \Sigma \frac{(-2)^2}{11} + \frac{(-3)^2}{11} + \frac{(-2)^2}{11} + \frac{(7)^2}{11}$$

$$x^2 = \frac{66}{11} = 6$$

Since a χ^2 value of 6 is less than 7.82, you must accept the null hypothesis. That means it is equally likely there will be 4, 5, 6, or 7 games in a World Series. This is a very surprising result. Just by looking at the numbers, it appears that a 7-game world series is much more likely to occur. However, the statistical analysis points out that it is equally likely there will be a 4-, 5-, 6-, or 7-game world series. This points out the importance of using statistical methods, rather than just looking and seeing to determine whether there is a significant difference between the experimental and control data.

Chapter 7

Science Projects You Can Do

Now that you have read about statistics and statistical testing methods, you can try out what you have learned on one or more of the following projects or on a project of your own design.

For every project, you can use the statistical methods in this book to:

- Create a table or chart
- Create a frequency distribution
- Create a graph
- Find the average
- Find the standard deviation
- Calculate percentiles

In addition, after each project experiment is a series of questions that you can answer using hypothesis testing methods. Each project is just a starting point. There are many other questions you can answer and experiments you can try in each of the areas. Use your imagination and enjoy science!

1. Design an experiment to determine changes in the humidity of air. You can do this by creating a hygrometer, an instrument that measures humidity. Test the effects of humidity on strands of silk thread, cotton thread, and wool.

   Use hypothesis testing to answer the following questions:

   • Is there a difference in hygroscopic action between the cotton and silk threads?

   • Is there a difference in hygroscopic action between the cotton and wool threads? Between the silk and wool threads?

2. Design an experiment to determine the effects that laundry detergent enzymes have on protein molecules.

Design an experiment that you think you will enjoy doing.

Hard-boiled eggs are one good source of protein molecules.

Use hypothesis testing to answer the following questions:

- Does the concentration of laundry detergent affect the results? Try different amounts of detergent such as 1 teaspoon, 1 tablespoon, 3 tablespoons, and so on.

- How do different laundry detergents compare in their ability to clean stains from cloth?

3. Design an experiment to determine whether adding nutrients to seeds speeds their germination. Standard fertilizers are a good source of added nutrients.

Use hypothesis testing to answer the following questions:

- Is there a difference in germination speed if you use different commercial fertilizer products?

- Is there a difference in speed of germination if the seeds are planted in different types of soils?

- Do different types of seeds (grass seed, beans) germinate at different speeds?

4. Design an experiment to determine how water affects seed germination.

Use hypothesis testing to answer the following questions:

- Does temperature have an effect on germination?

- Does light have an effect on germination?

- Does planting depth have an effect on germination?

5. Design an experiment to determine whether some soils erode faster than others.

Use hypothesis testing to answer the following questions:

- Does the speed of watering (the daily amount of rainfall) affect the speed of soil erosion in different soils?

- Does length of watering time (rainfall) affect the speed of soil erosion in different soils?

- Does the slope of the land affect the speed of soil erosion?

6. Design an experiment to determine whether vinegar is necessary for dyeing eggshells.

    Use hypothesis testing to answer the following questions:

    - Is the intensity of the color of the egg affected by the concentration of vinegar in the dye solution?

    - Does the temperature of the solution affect the results?

    - Does the color of the dye affect the results?

7. Design an experiment to see whether plants can be

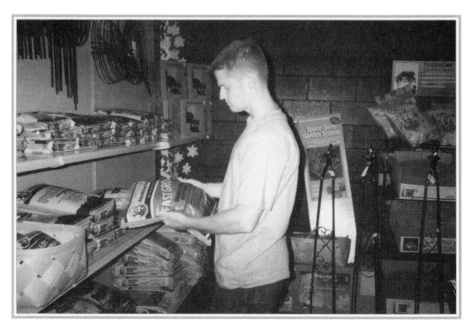

How fast does grass seed start growing when compared to the germination of different types of seeds?

grown without soil in a nutrient solution, that is, using hydroponics.

Use hypothesis testing to answer the following questions:

- Does the amount of sunlight received by the plants affect their growth?

- Does the amount of oxygen received by the plants affect their growth?

- Does the growing medium affect the growth of hydroponically grown plants?

8. Design an experiment to test the viscosity of a liquid, such as water. You can do this by building a viscometer, an instrument that measures the flow rate of liquids.

Use hypothesis testing to answer the following questions:

- Does the temperature of the water affect its viscosity?

- How does the viscosity of other liquids compare with the viscosity of water? Try liquids such as syrup, oil, dishwashing liquid, and so on.

- Does the viscosity of a liquid affect its stickiness?

- Does temperature affect the viscosity of the different liquids?

9. Design an experiment to grow sucrose crystals in a gelatin solution.

Use hypothesis testing to answer the following questions:

- Does temperature affect crystal formation? Is there a difference in the sugar crystal formation if the solution is cooled at a slower rate by insulating the jar?

- Does evaporation rate affect crystal formation? Place the gelatin mixture in containers with different surface areas for evaporation.

- Does purity of solution affect crystal formation?
  Mix several types of sugar together in the gelatin
  solution.

10. Design an experiment to demonstrate the transportation
    of liquid through a plant's vascular system.

    Use hypothesis testing to answer the following questions:

    - Does the presence of leaves on a stem affect the rate
      of translocation?

    - How does humidity affect the rate of transpiration?

    - Does the amount of light affect the rate of
      translocation?

    - Does the amount of light affect the rate of
      transpiration?

Science Projects Using Statistics

Statistics is not just a mathematical exercise. It helps produce
conclusions on some very important real-world issues. To give
you an idea of the kinds of problems they have helped solve,
a list of projects that high school students have done using the
methods explained in this book follows. These were indepen-
dent research projects submitted to science fair competitions.
The description of each project is the abstract of the write-up
submitted by the student.

A Study of the Possible Relationship Between Grade Point Average, Gender, and Logic Testing Technique and Ability

A mathematical logic problem and its solution (Emmet 1972)
were given to high school students. Nothing regarding the
presence of the solution set was explained to the students. It

was found that women viewed the solution sets as verification. Men viewed them as answers to be copied.

The Effects of the Algae *Codium fragile* Used as a Fertilizer on the Growth of Plants: A Two-Year Study

The algae *Codium fragile* was used as a plant fertilizer on fava beans and corn. The *Codium fragile* was prepared in two different ways: (1) dried powder form, (2) boiling and then dissolving in solution. Ortho Houseplant Food was used on a third group as a control. A fourth group received no fertilizer at all. It was found that there was no difference between the *Codium fragile* (either dried or boiled) and the Ortho Houseplant Food.

Phonological Revision Strategies in Young Children

This study examined the way that children make phonological repairs on their language when they perceive that they are not understood by an adult listener.

Is *Bacillus thurengensis israelensis* a Threat to Crustaceans Such as *Artemia salina*?

This study investigated the effects of *Bacillus thurengensis israelensis (Bti)* on *Artemia salina*. The study was based on the hypothesis that *Bti* is not harmful to *Artemia salina* regardless of concentration. *Artemia salina* were exposed to *Bti* concentrations of 0.01, 0.10, and 1.00 grams per 3 liters. Through statistical analysis it was shown that those *Artemia salina* exposed to the lower concentrations were unaffected, whereas those exposed to the higher concentrations experienced significantly higher mortality rates.

An Analysis of Ball Clay Pipe Fragments from the Terry-Mulford Site, Orient, New York

This project was an analysis of the ball clay pipe fragments recovered from the Terry-Mulford site in Orient, New York. Harrington's (1954) date/bore size correlation chart, Binford's (1961) mean production date formula, and Hanson's (1969) modifications of the Binford formula, the distribution of stems around the site, and the frequencies of bowl designs were some of the factors used to increase our knowledge of this site and its position in history.

Implications of Birth Order

As the oldest of three brothers, I have always been interested in birth order. I created a survey that could show the different characteristics of the different birth orders. I used the χ^2 test to determine that there is a significant difference between the different birth orders.

The Relationship of Vegetation to Tide Levels in the Long Island Salt Marshes

The purpose of this project was to test the hypothesis that vegetation can reliably be used as an indicator of tide data levels and salt marsh boundaries. Using information from the National Oceanographic and Atmospheric Administration, the vertical distance data was normalized for mean high water.

Hydrogeochemistry of the Peconic River

This project studied the chemical content of the Peconic River to determine seasonal and spatial variations in a very unpolluted and undeveloped area. Water was sampled at seven sites along the river. An ion chromatograph was used to determine the concentrations of three anions: chloride (Cl^-), nitrate (NO_3^-), and sulfate (SO_4^{--}).

Cheating in High School: Definition, Extent, and Causes

This study attempted to assess cheating behavior and attitudes in a suburban high school and relate them to several variables, including parental pressure, course level, and gender. It was found that 93 percent of students admitted to having committed, at least once, what are considered by the administration to be major cheating infractions. A one percent level of significance was used to test the variables.

An Investigation of the Motivations and Pressures of Secondary Students in a Music Conservatory Preparatory Program

The objective of this project was to learn more about the backgrounds and motivations of musically-talented youth. This goal was attained via the use of an anonymous survey and personal interviews that were given to students at the Pre-College Division of the Juilliard School of Music in New York City. Such topics as personal, peer, and parental pressures, and relationships, ethnic background, socioeconomic status, and personal views on academics, music, and future career plans were addressed in the survey and the interviews.

The Effects of Family on the Decision Making Processes of American and Japanese Students in a Moral Dilemma Paradigm

This study attempted to place American and Japanese students in a moral dilemma situation and compare the extent to which the family influenced how the students responded. It was found that Japanese students were influenced more by their family in making decisions than were American students.

Gender Difference in Everyday Knowledge

It has been found in other studies that women generally know less than men about politics. Since there are no significant differences in intelligence between men and women, the gender gap in political knowledge has been explained by differing social expectations for men and women. Politics has been described as a "male" area. In the last twenty years there has been change in American attitudes toward how men and women should behave. This study was done to see if the gender gap in political knowledge still exists among male and female teenagers today.

Lyme Disease in Cattle: Characterization of the Immune Response and Evaluation of Serological Testing

Bovine sera from four states all had antibodies to the Lyme disease bacterium (*Borrelia burgdorferi*) as determined by enzyme-linked immunosorbent assays. Certain of these cows with varying degrees of antibody reactivity were selected to have Western blots performed on them. Blot patterns from endemic and nonendemic areas were similar, suggesting the immune response was not necessarily due to *Borrelia burgdorferi*. There was no correlation between amounts of antibody and the number of total bands for bovines used in this study.

Chapter 8

Internet Resources

This book provided you with all the information needed to analyze and interpret the data that you collected while working on your research projects. This section contains a list of Web sites, as well as key words related to the material found in each of the chapters. The key words can be used with an Internet search engine to help you find additional information.

However, it is important to keep in mind that due to the rapidly evolving nature of the Internet, new resources appear daily. At the same time, some links become unavailable, while others will have their content radically modified.

Key Words

The following key words brought up many Internet sites when used with a conventional search engine. However, if you still need more information, check out the index for other key words.

The Internet can be a useful resource when working with statistics.

scientific method

central tendency

descriptive statistics

percentiles

inferential statistics

measures of variability

frequency distribution

standard deviation

class intervals

range

graphs

interquartile range

histogram

normal distribution

pie chart

correlation coefficient

stem-and-leaf diagrams

hypothesis testing

box plots

statistical test

Boxplots and Five-Number Summaries

http://dev1.epsb.edmonton.ab.ca/math14_Jim/math8/strand 4/4103.htm http://exploringdata.cqu.edu.au/boxplots.htm

The five-number summary includes the minimum and maximum values along with the quartiles to quickly summarize a distribution.

Central Tendency

http://www.courses.ncsu.edu/classes/psy242001/psy240/l17central/index.html

http://www.shodor.org/interactivate/lessons/st4.html

http://www.animatedsoftware.com/statglos/sgmean.htm

These Web sites contain solved problems as well as interactive activities to help you understand the differences between mean, median, and mode.

Class Intervals

http://www.shodor.org/interactivate/discussions/sd2.html

http://daphne.palomar.edu/stat/wpclassinterval.html

These sites contain several worked examples to help you create and understand class intervals.

Correlation Coefficient

Pearson r *for cardinal data*

http://noppa5.pc.helsinki.fi/koe/corr/cor1.html

http://davidmlane.com/hyperstat/A51911.html

Spearman rank correlation coefficient r *for ordinal data*

http://mathworld.wolfram.com/SpearmanRankCorrelationCoefficient.html

Data Sets

http://lib.stat.cmu.edu/DASL/

http://lib.stat.cmu.edu/datasets

http://www.fedstats.gov

http://www.whitehouse.gov

> *Several sites contain data from a wide variety of topics so that you can find real-world statistical examples.*

Descriptive and Inferential Statistics

http://glass.ed.asu.edu/stats/lesson0/

Descriptive Statistics

http://www.mste.uiuc.edu/hill/dstat/dstat.html

http://www.math.gatech.edu/~bourbaki/1700/
DescriptiveStatistics/Statistics.html

http://www.ifigure.com/math/stat/descript.htm

Electronic Statistical Journals

http://www.stats.gla.ac.uk/cti/links_stats/journals.html

http://www.amstat.org/publications/asajournals.html

> *These sites contain links to professional research journals. They list the titles of most of the other journals that you can find on the Internet.*

The American Statistical Society

http://www.stat.ncsu.edu/stated/

Journal of Statistics Education

http://www.stat.unipg.it/ncsu/info/jse/homepage.html

Chance News

http://www.dartmouth.edu/~chance/chance_news/news.html

Frequency Distribution

http://mathworld.wolfram.com/FrequencyDistribution.html

http://www.yale.edu/ynhti/curriculum/units/1986/5/86.05.03.x.html#d

http://www.psychstat.smsu.edu/introbook/sbk07m.htm

http://www.uop.edu/cop/psychology/Statistics/Class_interval.html

> *These sites define frequency distributions and give working examples to help you create your own frequency distributions.*

Graphs

http://library.thinkquest.org/10030/2srodg.htm

> *This is a site dedicated to describing all types of statistical graphs. There are many other sites in the following few paragraphs that describe specific types of graphs.*

Stem-and-Leaf Diagrams

http://davidmlane.com/hyperstat/A28117.html

http://psyc.queensu.ca/~flanagan/202_1999/lecture4/lecture4.html

Histograms

http://www.stat.sc.edu/~west/javahtml/Histogram.html

http://www.ajdcomputing.com/rachel/histmaker

These sites contain Java applets that allow you to interactively create and interpret your own data in the form of a histogram.

Frequency Polygons

http://www.uop.edu/cop/psychology/Statistics/fpolygon.html
http://mathworld.wolfram.com/FrequencyPolygon.html
http://davidmlane.com/hyperstat/A49236.html
http://daphne.palomar.edu/stat/wpfreqpoly.html

These sites contain several worked examples.

Pie Charts

http://www.shodor.org/interactivate/activities/piechart/

Pie charts are very useful for describing data. This site will help you create your own pie charts for your experimental data.

Hypothesis Testing

http://www.ruf.rice.edu/~lane/hyperstat/logic_hypothesis.html
http://www.westgard.com/lesson37.htm

One-Tailed and Two-Tailed Tests

http://www.statpac.com/surveys/statistical-significance.htm

Hypothesis tests can be broken up into one- and two-tailed versions. This site gives examples about both.

Inferential Statistics

http://149.170.199.144/resdesgn/inferent.htm
http://www.davidmlane.com/hyperstat/A29136.html

These sites give a general description about inferential statistics as well as worked examples.

Measures of Variability

http://www.stat.psu.edu/~resources/ClassNotes/ljs_12/sld001.htm

http://www.davidmlane.com/hyperstat/desc_univ.html

These sites define and give working examples about these measures.

Range and Interquartile Range

http://www.animatedsoftware.com/statglos/sgrange.htm

http://www.wabash.edu/depart/psych/Courses/Psych_2-3/Definitions/Ranges.htm

Standard Deviation

http://davidmlane.com/hyperstat/A16252.html

http://www.contingencyanalysis.com/glossarystandarddeviation.htm

http://www.animatedsoftware.com/statglos/sgstdev.htm

Normal Distribution

http://www.ruf.rice.edu/~lane/hyperstat/normal_distribution.html

This site describes the bell-shaped curve known as the normal curve.

Doing the correct statistical analysis of your data is one of the last steps in putting together a terrific science project.

Online Course Materials and Texts

Emory University
http://www.cc.emory.edu/EMORY_CLASS/PSYCH230/psych230.html

National Center on Education and the Economy
http://www.shodor.org/interactivate/lessons/index.html

Rice University
http://www.davidmlane.com/hyperstat/index.html

Southwest Missouri State University
http://www.psychstat.smsu.edu/introbook/sbk00.htm

Stephen Wolfram and Mathematica

http://mathworld.wolfram.com/topics/
ProbabilityandStatistics.html

Online Java Statistics Demonstrations

http://www.math.uah.edu/stat/hypothesis/hypothesis7.html
http://www.stat.duke.edu/sites/java.html
http://www.ruf.rice.edu/~lane/stat_sim/index.html
http://members.aol.com/johnp71/javastat.html

> *These sites present simulations for many of the statistical ideas presented in this book.*

Percentile and Percentile Rank

http://www.ux1.eiu.edu/~cfwdr/M&E-percentilerank.html

Statistics Competition

Poster Competition K–12

http://www.amstat.org/education/poster1.html

Project Competition 3–12

http://www.amstat.org/education/project.html

> *These sites contain information about two competitions supported by the American Statistical Association (ASA). Students can enter a poster or a project competition. Winners receive cash awards and ASA certificates for their efforts.*

The Scientific Method

http://pc65.frontier.osrhe.edu/hs/science/hsimeth.htm
http://biology.clc.uc.edu/courses/bio104/sci_meth.htm

http://phyun5.ucr.edu/~wudka/Physics7/Notes_www/
node5.html

Statistics Glossary

http://www.stats.gla.ac.uk/steps/glossary/index.html
  This glossary contains definitions for all statistical terms.

Statistics Resources

http://library.thinkquest.org/10030/statcon.htm
http://www.statistics.com
http://www.stats.gla.ac.uk/cti/links_stats/index.html
http://www.stat.ufl.edu/vlib/statistics.html
  *These sites are comprehensive guides to the most commonly
  used statistics resources on the Web. The sites contain software
  information, shareware, statistical analysis, computer-based
  learning projects, mailing lists, newsgroups, journals,
  textbooks, publishers, data sources, and simulations.*

Statistical Tests

http://www.med.umkc.edu/tlwbiostats/choosetest.html
http://mathworld.wolfram.com/topics/StatisticalTests.html
  *These sites provide an outline of the factors relevant to the
  choice of statistical tests. The first site includes a set of three
  charts that may be used to guide your selection of a test.*

T- test

http://vassun.vassar.edu/~lowry/VassarStats.html
  *The t-test requires that you know the sample mean, the
  sample standard deviation, and the population mean.*

Chi-square

http://www.georgetown.edu/cball/webtools/web_chi.html
http://courses.ncsu.edu/classes/psy242001/psy242/l17_nom/2x2.htm

> *When you are interested in comparing the distribution of data from a sample against a theoretical distribution in which each piece of data has the same probability of occurring you should use the chi-square test. The chi-square test answers the following question: How well does the observed distribution fit the theoretical distribution?*

Appendix A

Statistical Calculators

Solving statistical problems with just pencil and paper can often be a tedious task. Even if you understand the formulas, using them may be complicated and cumbersome when you have collected large amounts of data in a science research project. The following tools can help you perform your calculations.

Scientific Calculators

A scientific calculator can simplify working with large amounts of data. These calculators can be purchased for as little as twenty dollars. They can quickly sum columns of data, an operation frequently required in statistical formulas.

Most scientific and graphing calculators also come preprogrammed with many statistical functions. Several of the important keys to look for when buying a calculator to use for statistical purposes are:

$\bar{x}$	sample mean
μ	population mean
σ or σ_n	population standard deviation
σ_{n-1} or s	sample standard deviation
ρ	population correlation coefficient
r	sample correlation coefficient

Scientific calculators are not difficult to use. A little practice with the instruction book will save you many hours of pencil-and-paper work.

Computer Programs

Another time saver is statistical software packages. These programs are simple and easy to use. Most people can load them and begin using them immediately.

A computer program will do much more than the scientific calculator. In addition to finding the values for descriptive statistics, such as the mean, standard deviation, and correlation, statistical programs will allow you to determine whether the data you have collected is statistically significant.

The programs come with many statistical tests for inferential statistics, such as the t-test. Many of them also have the ability to create charts, tables, and graphs of your data.

Appendix B

Special Symbols and Formulas

Statistical formulas are filled with many symbols. However, most of the symbols are simply upper (capital) and lowercase Greek letters.

Using Σ

The Σ symbol is found in many statistical formulas. This symbol, the uppercase Greek letter sigma, is a summation symbol. It is a shorthand way of saying, "Add up all the numbers."

Suppose you were given 10 biology quizzes in which the highest possible score was 10. If you listed the scores in your notebook, they might look something like this:

Biology quizzes: 8, 3, 5, 9, 7, 8, 6, 4, 10, 8

You would probably give them some kind of title like the one shown so that you could identify them later. For convenience, statisticians identify their data with mathematical symbols instead of titles. Quite often, their title is a single letter. They might change your title to Q for quiz, but most likely, they would call it x for unknown. In that case, your list would look like this:

x: 8, 3, 5, 9, 7, 8, 6, 4, 10, 8

This gives us the same information, but in a much more condensed form. You can now use the title much more easily with the summation symbol. Suppose you want to say, "Add up all 10 quiz values." In mathematical form, that would look like this:

$$\Sigma x$$

$$\Sigma x = 8 + 3 + 5 + 9 + 7 + 8 + 6 + 4 + 10 + 8 = 68$$

Other Statistical Symbols

Some other common symbols that are found in statistical formulas are listed below.

1. μ represents the population mean. It is the lowercase Greek letter mu, pronounced "moo."

2. $\bar{x}$ represents the sample mean. It is read "x bar."

3. σ represents the population standard deviation. It is the lowercase Greek letter sigma.

4. σ_{n-1} or s represents the sample standard deviation.

5. ρ represents the population correlation coefficient. It is the lowercase Greek letter rho, pronounced "row."

6. r represents the sample correlation coefficient.

7. N or n represents the number of pieces of data that have been collected in the experiment.

8. χ^2 represents the relative squared difference between a population frequency and a sample frequency. χ^2 is the lowercase Greek letter chi, pronounced "ky" and χ^2 is the tested value in the chi-square test used in hypothesis testing.

Using Statistical Formulas

Mathematical formulas are just a way of writing complicated ideas in mathematical shorthand. Two of the most often used statistical formulas are shown below.

The Mean

The formula to find the mean is:

$$\bar{x} = \frac{\sum x}{n}$$

This formula says that to find the value of the mean:

1. Sum up the data values.

2. Divide the sum by the quantity of your data values.

A complete explanation of the mean is found in Chapter 2.

The Standard Deviation

The formula for calculating the standard deviation for a sample is:

$$s = \sqrt{\frac{\sum (x - \bar{x})^2}{n-1}}$$

This formula says that to find the value of the standard deviation:

1. Find the value of the mean.

2. Subtract the mean from every data value.

3. Square each difference.

4. Sum up these squared differences.

5. Divide the sum by the number of data values minus 1.

6. Find the square root of the entire calculation.

A complete explanation of the use and meaning of the standard deviation is given in Chapter 3.

Other Formulas Used in this Book

The formula for percentile rank (PR):

$$P.R. = \frac{cum\ f}{n} \times 100$$

The formula for the range:

$$Range = Maximum - Minimum$$

The formula for the interquartile range (IQR):

$$IQR = Q_3 - Q_1$$

The formula for the Pearson r correlation coefficient:

$$r = \frac{\Sigma xy - \frac{1}{n} \Sigma x\, \Sigma y}{\sqrt{(\Sigma x^2 - \frac{(\Sigma x)^2}{n})\, (\Sigma y^2 - \frac{(\Sigma y)^2}{n})}}$$

The formula for the z-test:

$$z = \frac{\bar{x} - \mu}{\frac{\sigma}{\sqrt{n}}}$$

The formula for the t-test:

$$t = \frac{\bar{x} - \mu_0}{\frac{s}{\sqrt{n}}}$$

The formula for the ρ-test:

$$t = \frac{r\sqrt{n-2}}{\sqrt{1-r^2}}$$

The formula for the chi-square test:

$$\chi^2 = \Sigma\frac{(f_o - f_e)^2}{f_e}$$

Appendix C

Tables of Critical Values

Table I. Critical values of z

.01 one-tail	.05 one-tail	.01 two-tail	.05 two-tail
2.33	1.65	2.58	1.96

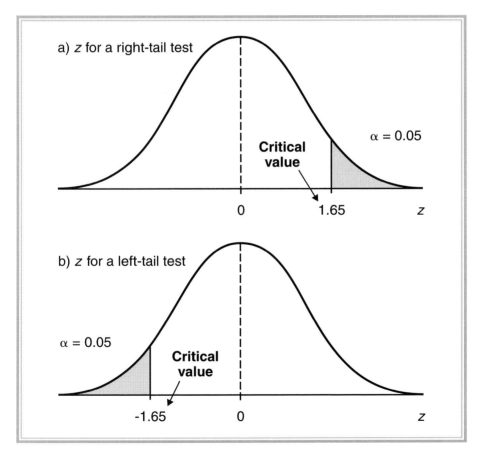

a) *z* for a right-tail test

Critical value

$\alpha = 0.05$

0   1.65   *z*

b) *z* for a left-tail test

$\alpha = 0.05$

Critical value

-1.65   0   *z*

Figure i: A one-tail value can be either positive (a) or negative (b).

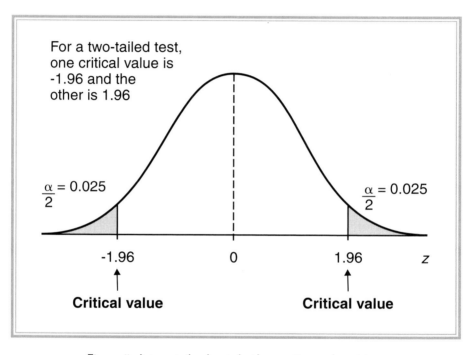

For a two-tailed test, one critical value is -1.96 and the other is 1.96

$\frac{\alpha}{2} = 0.025$

$\frac{\alpha}{2} = 0.025$

-1.96

0

1.96

z

↑
Critical value

↑
Critical value

Figure ii: A two-tail value is both negative and positive.

Table II: Upper-tail critical values of *t*
(Note: The lower-tail critical value is the negative value of the upper-tail critical value.)

df	.01 one-tail	.05 one-tail	.01 two-tail	.05 two-tail
5	3.37	2.02	4.03	2.57
6	3.14	1.94	3.71	2.45
7	3.00	1.90	3.50	2.37
8	2.90	1.86	3.36	2.31
9	2.82	1.83	3.25	2.26
10	2.76	1.81	3.17	2.23
11	2.71	1.80	3.11	2.20
12	2.68	1.78	3.06	2.18
13	2.65	1.77	3.01	2.16
14	2.62	1.76	2.98	2.15
15	2.60	1.75	2.95	2.13
16	2.58	1.75	2.92	2.12
17	2.57	1.74	2.90	2.11
18	2.55	1.73	2.88	2.10
19	2.54	1.73	2.86	2.09
20	2.53	1.73	2.85	2.09
21	2.52	1.72	2.83	2.08
22	2.51	1.72	2.82	2.07
23	2.50	1.71	2.81	2.07
24	2.49	1.71	2.80	2.06
25	2.49	1.71	2.79	2.06
30	2.48	1.70	2.75	2.04
40	2.42	1.68	2.70	2.02
60	2.39	1.67	2.66	2.00
120	2.36	1.66	2.62	1.98
∞	2.33	1.65	2.58	1.96

Table III: Critical values of χ^2

df	.01	.05
1	6.64	3.84
2	9.21	5.99
3	11.34	7.82
4	13.28	9.49
5	15.09	11.07
6	16.81	12.59
7	18.48	14.07
8	20.09	15.51
9	21.67	16.92
10	23.21	18.31
15	30.58	25.00
20	37.57	31.41
25	44.31	37.65
30	50.89	43.77

Appendix D

General Guidelines for Hypothesis Testing

One of the most difficult judgments you have to make in hypothesis testing is which statistical test to use for your given data. The guidelines listed below will help you make your decision.

The Z-Test

Use this test when:

- You know the mean, μ, and standard deviation, σ, for the population.

- The underlying distribution is the standard normal curve. This is usually true for large populations.

Look up critical values for the z-test in Table I in Appendix C. To calculate z:

$$z = \frac{\bar{x} - \mu}{\dfrac{\sigma}{\sqrt{n}}}$$

The T-Test

Use this test when:

- The population mean, μ, and sample standard deviation, s, are known.

- The underlying distribution is a family of curves that vary according to the number of degrees of freedom, a statistic related to the size of the sample.

Look up critical values for the t-test in Appendix Table II using $df = n - 1$. To calculate t:

$$t = \frac{\bar{x} - \mu_0}{\dfrac{s}{\sqrt{n}}}$$

The Rho Test

Use this test when:

- The sample correlation coefficient, r, is known.

- You want to know whether your sample comes from a population in which the correlation coefficient is 0.00.

Look up the critical value for the ρ-test in Appendix Table II using $df = n - 2$.

The formula for the ρ-test is:

$$t = \frac{r\sqrt{n - 2}}{\sqrt{1 - r^2}}$$

Chi-Square (χ^2) Test

Use this test when:

- You want to know how well the observed distribution fits the theoretical distribution.

Look up critical values for the χ^2 test in Appendix Table III. To calculate χ^2:

$$\chi^2 = \Sigma \frac{(f_o - f_e)^2}{f_e}$$

The Method

A good practice in any hypothesis testing is to follow these general steps:

1. Summarize the known facts.

2. Establish the alternative hypothesis.

3. Establish the null hypothesis.

4. Choose the level of significance.

5. Choose the appropriate test statistic (z, t, χ^2, or ρ) for your problem.

6. Create a geometric model of your distribution.

7. Identify the critical value and the critical region.

8. Calculate the value of the test statistic.

9. Formulate a conclusion.

Glossary

alternative hypothesis—The hypothesis that says there is a difference between the sample statistic and the population parameter.

average—The center of a set of data. Defines the mean (also known as the average), median, or mode of the data.

bar graph—A graph consisting of vertical or horizontal bars whose lengths represent the number of items in a category.

bimodal—Describes a distribution that has two modes.

boxplot—A pictorial representation of a five-number summary.

class interval—Groups the data into separate categories to give an indication of the distribution of scores.

class mark—The midpoint of a class interval.

correlation—A relationship between two variables observed from the same subject.

correlation coefficient—A value between −1 and 1 that indicates the degree of relationship between two variables.

critical value—The value in hypothesis testing that determines whether the statistician accepts or rejects the null hypothesis. The location of the test statistic with respect to the critical value determines which decision will be made.

cumulative frequency *(cum f)*—The sum of all the frequencies of data values from the lowest class interval up to and including a given class. When divided by the total number of data values and multiplied by 100, it is equivalent to the percentile rank.

data—The numbers collected and worked with during a

research project. Some examples are: the number of French fries in a fast-food serving; your town's daily rainfall in inches; the age of Americans who have had heart transplants; and the height of sixteen-year-old girls in the United States.

decile—A grouping of percentiles into 10 groups of 10 percentile points each.

degrees of freedom—The size of the sample minus one.

descriptive statistic—A measurable characteristic of data. Some examples are mean, range, percentile rank, standard deviation, and correlation.

distribution—The way the data is spread over a range of values.

five-number summary—A list of five numbers consisting of the minimum value, the quartiles, and the maximum value from a data set.

frequency—The total number of times that a measurement or category occurs in a collection of data. The symbol f is used to denote the frequency of a measurement.

frequency distribution—An arrangement of data that reveals how it clusters at various values. It offers an indication of how frequently the data appears in each section of a graph or table.

frequency polygon—A graph made by connecting the midpoints of the class intervals.

histogram—A graph consisting of bars whose length represents the number of items within a class interval. In contrast to a bar graph, the width of each bar represents a numerical value and the bars always touch.

hypothesis—A hypothesis is a statement asserting the problem you will be investigating in your experiment. Some examples are: Is the average age of heart transplant recipients getting younger? Are sixteen-year-old girls taller today than they were in 1956?

hypothesis testing—A procedure statisticians use to test a hypothesis in order to determine whether data from a sample is representative of the entire population.

inferential statistics—Allow the researcher to make inferences about a population from studying a small portion, or sample, from it. Some examples of inferential statistics are the z-test statistic, the t-test statistic, and the p-test statistic.

interquartile range—The difference between the first and third quartile in a data set.

level of significance—The probability of obtaining a type I error in hypothesis testing. It is a number the statistician chooses as an acceptable risk of error.

linear—Having a straight-line relationship.

mean—The average of a group of data values found by dividing their sum by the number of values.

median—The value of the central piece of data in a data set.

midpoint—The value in the center of a group of data.

mode—The value of the piece of data that occurs most often in a data set.

multimodal—A distribution having more than two modes.

normal distribution—A frequency distribution that when plotted has a symmetrical bell shape, with the mean in the center and a specific standard deviation. This distribution is common for large sets of data.

null hypothesis—The hypothesis that says there is no difference between the sample value and the population value.

one-tailed test—A hypothesis test in which the rejection region is on only one side of the mean. In the geometric model, the rejection region is in only one tail of the distribution.

outlier—A piece of data that is located far away from the rest of the data values.

parameter—A measurable characteristic of a population. Some examples are: the average age of all the people in the United States who have had a heart transplant, and the average height of all sixteen-year-old girls in the United States.

Pearson *r* correlation coefficient formula—The formula for calculating the amount of linear correlation between two variables.

percentile rank—The percentage of data that is equal to or less than a given value.

population—All the individuals or objects with a common observable characteristic. Some examples are: all the people in the United States who have had a heart transplant, and the average height of all sixteen-year-old girls in the United States. See *sample*.

probability—The chance that an event will occur as a fraction of 1, with 1 indicating it will definitely occur.

quartile—Breaks the range of percentiles into quarters.

random sample—A sample selected in such a way that every member of the population shares an equal chance of being selected.

range—The difference between the greatest and smallest values in a set of data.

sample—A small group or subset of the population. Some examples of samples are: the people who have had heart transplants at your local hospital, or the sixteen-year-old girls in the tenth grade at your high school. See *population*.

skewed—Not symmetric; slanted in one direction.

standard deviation—A measure of the dispersion of data around the mean in a data set. In other words, it is a calculation that indicates how far the data values tend to deviate from the mean.

standard normal curve—The plot of a normal distribution in which the mean has been set to zero and the standard deviation has been set to 1.

statistic—A measurable characteristic of a sample. Some examples are: the people who have had heart transplants at your local hospital, and the sixteen-year-old girls in the tenth grade at your high school. See *population.*

statistical significance—The determination of whether a finding about a sample of data from a research project is valid from a statistical point of view.

student's *t* distribution—A frequency distribution that occurs with small sample sizes. It changes shape with sample size, and at large sample sizes it resembles the normal distribution.

symmetric—Describes a graph or set of values in which one half is a mirror image of the other half.

true limits—The upper and lower bounds of a measurement. The true limits of a number are equal to the number plus and minus 1/2 of the measuring unit.

two-tailed test—A hypothesis test in which the rejection region is on both sides of the mean. In the geometric model, the rejection region is in both tails of the distribution.

type I error—The error that occurs in hypothesis testing when a hypothesis that is actually true is rejected as false.

type II error—The error that occurs in hypothesis testing when a hypothesis that is actually false is accepted as true.

whiskers—Lines to the minimum and maximum values in a boxplot.

Further Reading

Ehrlich, Robert. *Nine Crazy Ideas in Science: A Few Might Even Be True.* N.J.: Princeton University Press, 2001.

Krieger, Melanie Jacobs. *How to Excel in Science Competitions, Revised and Updated.* Berkeley Heights, N.J.: Enslow Publishers, Inc., 1999.

Robinson, Tom Mark. *The Everything Kids' Science Experiments Book: Boil Ice, Float Water, Measure Gravity—Challenge the World Around You!* Avon, Mass.: Adams Media Corporation, 2001.

Slavin, Stephen L. *Chances Are: The Only Statistics Book You'll Ever Need.* Lanham, Md.: Madison Books, Inc., 1998.

Vecchione, Glen. *100 Award-Winning Science Fair Projects.* New York: Sterling Publishing Company, Inc., 2001.

Index